Confessions of a
Professional
Mourner

Confessions of a
Professional
Mourner

Lisa D. Putnam

XULON PRESS

Xulon Press
2301 Lucien Way #415
Maitland, FL 32751
407.339.4217
www.xulonpress.com

© 2020 by Lisa D. Putnam

All rights reserved solely by the author. The author guarantees all contents are original and do not infringe upon the legal rights of any other person or work. No part of this book may be reproduced in any form without the permission of the author. The views expressed in this book are not necessarily those of the publisher.

Unless otherwise indicated, Scripture quotations taken from the New King James Version (NKJV). Copyright © 1982 by Thomas Nelson, Inc. Used by permission. All rights reserved.

Scripture quotations taken from the New American Standard Bible (NASB). Copyright © 1960, 1962, 1963, 1968, 1971, 1972, 1973, 1975, 1977, 1995 by The Lockman Foundation. Used by permission. All rights reserved.

Scripture quotations taken from the Amplified Bible (AMP). Copyright © 1954, 1958, 1962, 1964, 1965, 1987 by The Lockman Foundation. Used by permission. All rights reserved.

Scripture quotations taken from The Message (MSG). Copyright © 1993, 1994, 1995, 1996, 2000, 2001, 2002. Used by permission of NavPress Publishing Group. Used by permission. All rights reserved.

Scripture quotations taken from the Holy Bible, New International Version (NIV). Copyright © 1973, 1978, 1984, 2011 by Biblica, Inc.™ Used by permission. All rights reserved.

Scripture quotations taken from the Holy Bible, New Living Translation (NLT). Copyright ©1996, 2004, 2007 by Tyndale House Foundation. Used by permission of Tyndale House Publishers, Inc.

Paperback ISBN-13: 978-1-6322-1268-9
Ebook ISBN-13: 978-1-6322-1269-6

Table of Contents

Acknowledgments vii
Foreword ix
Introduction xi

CHAPTER 1
My Friend Ruth 1

CHAPTER 2
The Cost of Comfort 13

CHAPTER 3
Rejecting Rejection 27

CHAPTER 4
Following Favor or Estrangement Entanglement 41

CHAPTER 5
From Preparation to Provision 53

CHAPTER 6
No Weeping, No Reaping 65

CHAPTER 7
Casting Away the Past for Anointed Substance 81

CHAPTER 8
Covered in Covenant 93

CHAPTER 9
At the Gate of Redemption 103

CHAPTER 10
A Blessed Lineage Restored 115

Bibliography 133

Acknowledgments

Paul, you have encouraged me like no other, patiently listening to my dreams and making them your own. You have been my secretary, my editor, and my sounding board. Even after the longest day of serving others, you took the time to serve me. Although this is written as my story, your fingerprints are all over it. Thank you for your faithfulness, love, and friendship for over thirty-five years. You are my delight!

Chloe, Keegan, Karlton, and Hadley, you are God's precious gifts to me! You each bless and influence me in the unique ways that you were created. I love each of you fiercely. You are my favorites!

Mom and Dad, your confidence in me is daunting. I will always appreciate your belief in me and affirmation that, with the Lord's help, I can accomplish what I desire. Thank you for always supporting me.

Deborah, Lynn, Noel, and Julie, my "Sistas," how many years have I threatened this book? Nevertheless, you have been my cheerleaders and sacred friends for many years—thank you. What would I do without you and all the laughter, tears and lasting friendship? Julie, thank you for the early edits and insight, bringing clarity to what I desired to communicate. Your help was invaluable!

Lisa, thank you for sharing your editing skills and counsel as I moved toward publication. You are my name twin and friend, and hopefully, there will be more projects together in the future.

Pastors Dan and Terry Hammer for nurturing me, pouring the oil of joy for mourning and making room in what seemed like a confined season.

Foreword

Lisa Putnam has written an amazing book about the book of Ruth in the Bible. I have known Lisa and her husband, Paul for many years. She is a godly woman, wife, mother, speaker, writer, Bible teacher, prayer warrior and more. I have observed her and her family over the years and seen their Christian heritage and example.

So what's "Confessions of a Professional Mourner" about? I am glad you asked! It is about the lessons found in the narrative of Ruth and Naomi's lives and interwoven with Lisa's personal life experiences. It can be used for an individual, a group, a bible study or devotional. Lisa does a masterful job of weaving the truths of Ruth's story into questions at the end of each chapter that can make us think and change our lives for the better. I reflected on my own life as I read the book and there is great application to everyday life. In other words, it is very practical.

All the chapters are great, but I personally loved two of them: Chapter 10-"A Blessed Lineage Restored" and Chapter 2-"The Cost of Comfort." They tell about how God can bless our lineage and how God can bless us "outside our comfort zone." I am sure you will find your own favorite chapters as you read. But again, they are all good chapters.

Read and enjoy! Apply it and watch your life change. Just as Boaz, Ruth's kinsmen redeemer; may Jesus, your Kinsmen Redeemer change your life through this book.

Dr. Dan C. Hammer
Sonrise Christian Center
Senior Apostolic Leader

Introduction

It was early afternoon, and to my surprise, I found myself sitting leisurely watching television, a rarity in my life with young children, but nap time and completed housework had aligned to afford me such a guilty pleasure. As the wife of a pastor and a mother of four children, I had an idea (probably more of a compulsion) to keep my home and those around me ordered in such a way that it left little time to relax. No one had put that on me; in fact, the church we served housed a congregation full of gracious individuals. It was something I put on myself, an expectation or a snapshot for others that I had it together. Or, maybe better explained; everything was under control. Little did I know that assumption was so wrong. I sat down on my comfy sofa and as I channel surfed, I "happened upon" (a theme we will focus on a little later) a teaching program on a Christian network. With the house quiet, I settled in to learn and just be encouraged about what was to be shared.

In the course of the message, the speaker casually referenced "professional mourners" in the Bible and explained briefly their place in culture at the time. They were hired by loved ones of a deceased person to cry and wail in order to properly mourn their loss. These hired mourners would stir up emotion without having any ties to the deceased individual, but they only had information about the circumstances surrounding their death.

It was in that moment that I became aware of something, a quickening in my spirit, and in a judgmental attitude I flippantly thought to myself, *I know someone like that; they are always upset about what they cannot change, making more of a situation than what is warranted even to the point of provoking emotions.* Then, right in the middle of my internal dialogue, the Lord spoke gently to my heart: "Yes, and you are one of them." Sweet conviction came, and as I confessed my sin through tears of repentance, I received healing for my broken heart.

So began my journey, the beginning of not only one but many confessions, but also much healing and freedom. It wasn't only in that moment, but over several years of peeling away layers of self-preservation that I thought had protected me. Remember my carefully ordered home? It was just a piece of what was really an armor of regret that kept me from walking in the liberty Jesus had secured for me on the Cross. Don't get me wrong; I am not saying there isn't godly sorrow or even mourning over various types of loss, especially the loss of a loved one. This book is my testimony of how God delivered me from various thought patterns that hindered growth in my life. I am speaking to the negative places we take that loss.

Sometimes we never let go in order to receive the healing and redemption the Lord has to offer. Even as I began to travel on this road, I would experience great loss, hurt, and grief. Difficulties in my marriage, challenges with children, disappointment in relationships, and realistic expectations that were never realized came and should have cemented this attitude, but because of God's amazing grace, they exposed my tendency to get stuck. Instead, I found myself walking through fields of mercy and onto paths ending in joyous purpose. The Lord even saw fit to give me a companion for this adventure—her name was Ruth.

Chapter 1
My Friend Ruth

I never really identified with the book of Ruth very much. Yes, I was aware of her story and heard her referenced many times at weddings with the lovely phrase, "Entreat me not to leave." Yet, I didn't realize how much of my "mournful" attitude was woven in her life and how much truth would apply to my situations. Ruth had experienced much loss, and she chose to walk forward through change. Even when she had loved ones around her, who could have easily pulled her down with their attitudes, she pushed onward. I needed a friend like that! I needed someone who, by example, would propel me toward faith and purpose. Now before we get into her story, let's take a look at a little history surrounding my testimony and thoughts.

Professional Mourning in History

Professional mourning in ancient civilizations was widely used and regarded as a critical part to a funeral. People were hired, mostly women, to weep, wail, and shriek loudly to adequately mourn an individual. Many saw it as organized grief, and it was used to help the coordinating of mourning, particularly for the wealthy. The more "mourners," the more affluence the family held, and the louder the funeral procession, the more honorable the loved one. They were similar to event planners or funeral directors today. As time went on, the practice eventually became frowned upon by many as being insincere.

Symbolically

In the Bible we see references to professional mourning in: Ecclesiastes 12:5; Jeremiah 9:17; Amos 5:16; and Matthew 9:23 (Jairus's daughter). They were called upon in many instances to mourn Israel's spiritual infidelity. For our purposes, we are going to view it symbolically with the idea that we experience loss of different kinds, which begins to color our view of life and our relationship with Father God. We may begin to see things through the eyes of crisis and loss as opposed to God's goodness (all things work together for good). We may stir up our emotions by dwelling on what has past or what may have been when healing is trying to take place.

It may be as simple as not leaving well enough alone; contemplating, trying to fix what we cannot, crying and continuing to be devastated over a situation that in the natural course of life has finished. It may be replaying a memory to the point that the influence of emotions has added or taken away from important scenes, distorting the event, or it may be leaving a picture no longer accurate but blurred from reality. It does not have to be overt but can be subtle in our attitudes, words, and especially in our thoughts, belaboring a longing and desire for the past glory days in the "way we were" syndrome. We can even develop an expectation for rejection—"Due to my circumstances, I am no longer lovely, acceptable, or deserving of God's goodness; this just must be my lot in life." Ultimately, this undermines our trust in God.

Confession *Is* Really Good for the Soul!

A big part of my healing and restoration came through the process of confession. However, it took me a while to understand how healthy it actually was. Perhaps I felt that if I kept my struggles quiet, they would disappear, or better yet, people would think I really had it all together. Beep, wrong answer! Unfortunately, I fooled no one but myself. Maybe we should take a look at what it means to "confess."

Confess (Strong's H 3034): *yadah*—to throw at or away, to revere or worship, intent to bemoan (by wringing of the hands), make confession. Merriam Webster's Dictionary adds: to unburden one's sins.

Let it sink in: to throw away, a wringing of the hands, be done with it. In other words, just let it go! Unburden your heavy heart! In fact, the Hebrew for this word implies to confess is part of an act of worship. Toss up your burdens to Him.

> *"³When I refused to confess my sin,*
> *my body wasted away,*
> *and I groaned all day long.*
> *⁴Day and night your hand of discipline was heavy on me.*
> *My strength evaporated like water in the summer heat. Interlude*
> *⁵Finally, I confessed* **all my sins to you**
> **and stopped trying to hide my guilt.**
> **I said to myself, "I will confess my rebellion to the Lord."**
> **And you forgave me! All my guilt is gone."** *Interlude*
> (Ps. 32:3, NLT)

I don't know about you but it is a lot easier for me to groan all day long than it is to just *confess* the issue. I revert to that self-willed toddler with an explanation of "I do it"! I can take care of myself, I know better, I can do better. I love watching my grandchildren, to see them growing and becoming independent. I can hear, "I do it," ringing in my ears even now. But there are times when that moment of freedom turns into, "Help, Nanny"! And I am more than happy to come alongside with assistance. Now I realize it is not a sin to do things on your own. But when it turns into weights that deplete our strength, it is our own self-reliance, and that can lead to pride, which is certainly a sin. Jesus wanted us to give Him our worries, cares, and burdens (Matt. 11:28), and it was His mission to save us. Let's take a look at one aspect of Psalm 32:3–5, highlighting verse 3b: *"I groaned all day long."*

Groaning (Strong's H584/585): *anachah*—to groan, mourn, or sigh. It is interesting that the word *complain* is defined in Webster's as: to express grief, pain, or discontent.

Do you see the contrast? When we confess, we release our burdens, and we express our need for Him, even if our "rebellion" is just trying to handle things our own way. Or, we may think our life situations are too minimal or simplistic for a mighty God to get involved. So let me ask you this, if a loved one asked you for help or expressed a weakness they needed direction for, would you deny them assistance? I had become accustomed to groaning, expressing my circumstances through complaining. Underneath it all was a deep sadness that my life was not turning out as I had expected. Worst of all, I really thought I had given myself to the Lord, which made it all feel somewhat of a betrayal.

Until *finally*. Why is it that we have to get to that "finally" place and allow God to do what was in His heart all along to really deliver us from ourselves? Because the alternative of replaying disappointing scenarios will eventually leave us with our "strength evaporated" and our faith depleted. We succumb to the pressure of unrealized expectations and allow them to mold our mind-sets instead of the Word of God. While we are forming our beliefs, He is waiting in the wings to comfort and bring peace to the turmoil in our spirits. He is waiting to lift us out of our despair.

We may think it is somewhat cathartic to express every emotion, but I have found that complaining results in physical and emotional consequences. If we're not careful, that vent will turn into a vow and commit us to something contrary to what God has planned. Our declarations, in the form of a complaint, will bind us to the very thing from which we desire relief or freedom. Some phrases that bring negative consequences are: This is the way I am, bad things always happen to me, no one likes me, or I'm not talented enough. Get the picture? If you are on the receiving end of such talk, you may wish to distance yourself from such a person, or you may feel like it's up to you to change things for that person, or worse, you may feel overwhelmed, not knowing what to do with it at all. On the other hand, confessing results in life. The Word of God gives us another tool. Instead of magnifying the negatives of life, the Bible encourages us in Psalm 34:3–4 (NKJV) to "magnify the Lord."

> *"Oh, magnify the LORD with me,*
> *And let us exalt His name together.*
> *⁴ I sought the LORD, and He heard me,*
> *And delivered me from all my fears."*

To *magnify* something is to make it greater or larger. To magnify the Lord above our circumstances brings the focus back to His greatness. I like to think of it as making Him so great that it pushes back everything else. Through our praise to a mighty God, we confront what is contrary to His character. Our adulation aligns our heart and mind with our Lord, who is our Deliverer. Then, our words bring our minds into agreement with His Word. It can go something like this:

Confession: "I feel like I'm alone."

Praise: "I thank and praise you Lord because your Word says that you will never leave me or forsake me" (Heb. 13:5).

It is also helpful to share our burdens with another person, and although our confession is most beneficial when we release it to the Lord, relationship with our spiritual family is part of God's plan to bring restoration.

In James 5:16 we are told:

> *Confess to one another therefore your faults (your slips, your false steps, your offenses, your sins) and pray [also] for one another, that you may be healed and restored [to a spiritual tone of mind and heart]. The earnest (heartfelt, continued) prayer of a righteous man makes*

tremendous power available [dynamic in its working]. (I love it in the Amplified Version.)

You see, not only do we confess, but then we pray—for each other. It's not belabored. No penance is needed; just care and concern approaching the Lord in a spiritual tone. No condescending, self-righteous tone is needed. It involves transparency in our trusted relationships. So much of my life was spent in trying to show everyone how perfectly I lived that it took some time to understand it was okay to be flawed. That doesn't mean we stay there or have an excuse to remain in our broken state. Jesus died to give us life and not just a diminished, so-so existence, but life abundant!

Let's look again at Psalm 34 and further through verses 1–6:

> *I will bless the Lord at all times;*
> *His praise shall continually be in my mouth.*
> *² My soul shall make its boast in the Lord;*
> *The humble shall hear of it and be glad.*
> *³ Oh, magnify the Lord with me,*
> *And let us exalt His name together.*
> *⁴ I sought the Lord, and He heard me,*
> *And delivered me from all my fears.*
> *⁵ They looked to Him and were radiant,*
> *And their faces were not ashamed.*
> *⁶ This poor man cried out, and the Lord heard him,*
> *And saved him out of all his troubles.*

Our worship can yield some very positive results, such as answers to prayer, deliverance from fear, and our mood and countenance lifted. He saves us from trouble. The biggest result of our worship is our focus changes from being self-absorbed to being immersed in the presence of God. As we look to Jesus, the Author and Finisher of our faith (Heb. 12:2), the source of our life; we are comforted by all that He endured and are encouraged by the victory He obtained. He is our perfect example of struggle, perseverance, and overcoming! This leads me to the book of Ruth and a brief historical back story.

Timeline and History

The book of Ruth was written somewhere between 1050 and 500 BC, and although the author is unknown, Jewish tradition holds it to the writings of Samuel. The predominant theme of the book points to God's sovereignty and His desire to intervene in order to bring about universal redemption. Ruth's story is a story about family, a family that made choices that turned out not to be the best for all involved.

"Now it came to pass, in the days when the judges ruled, that there was a famine in the land. And a certain man of Bethlehem, Judah, went to dwell in the country of Moab, he and his wife and his two sons: (Ruth 1:1). Elimelech led his family into a country that was flawed to say the least. As shameful as it is, the Moabites were a people resulting from an incestuous relationship between Lot (Abraham's nephew) and his older daughter. This occurred after Lot and his family was rescued from Sodom (Gen. 19:30). A few other instances to point out include:

- In the wilderness wanderings with Moses, the Israelites sought passage through Moab and God tells Israel to leave them alone (Deut. 2:7–9).

- The Moabites try to get Balaam to curse Israel, but God forces Balaam to bless them instead. (Num. 22:21–35).

- Due to these transgressions, Moab was excluded from the assembly (Deut. 23:3–5).

We open to the book of Ruth and read; "In the days when the judges ruled" (for the Lord raised up judges, Judg. 2:16). Even though God had brought His people through the wilderness into their inheritance and had given them the tabernacle of Moses, a functioning priesthood, and civil, moral, and religious laws, they continued to do what was right in their own eyes (Judg. 21:25). Sometimes we see courage and strength, and other times we see trouble. I see myself in this picture; no matter how many times God has intervened on my behalf, it is sometimes easier to revert to my old mind-set.

The example of Elimelech shows a returning to old company and surroundings. Perhaps he forgot about the renewing of the covenant at Moab when God reminds Israel how He took care of them in the wilderness and how their clothes and sandals remained intact for forty years (Deut. 29). Bethlehem means "house of bread," yet when famine came, Elimelech left the declared promise due to circumstances we don't know much about. Famine may have occurred because of a curse or a result of disobedience, but it is more likely due to an agricultural cycle. He showed tremendous disregard and contempt for his ancestors by fleeing to a country whose people were not only heathen but under a curse. Also, his family could have faced persecution just by residing there because of the Moabite's attitudes toward Israel in general. Most likely in his temporary hardship, Elimelech panicked and left his promise.

As we look closely as Ruth's life, we will see God's faithfulness to His people, as well as His desire to be inclusive of all people groups. Even within our panic and bad choices, He has a plan. It is a plan not only to redeem but also to restore, like the young couple that finds themselves pregnant before the wedding and they make the hard decision to choose life; later to fight for the unborn in society. Or the teenager who is running with the bad crowd ends up serving jail time but goes on to get an education in law and now serves as a judge, encouraging youth to walk a different path. God not only reaches back to what is lost, He looks forward to our future and sets us into eternity. What a loving and amazing God we serve!

Maybe right now you may be thinking, *That's great for her but how can my life be turned around*? Perhaps you think that your life is a representation of "Moab," and you are excluded from being a part of

God's family due to relationships or associations from your past? Take a moment and say this little prayer. I guarantee you, the price Jesus paid is greater and the journey will be worth it!

> Father God, I come to You now, and I confess that Your plans are greater than my plans; and Your thoughts are higher than my thoughts. I choose to trust You in all things, and where you lead I will follow.
>
> In Jesus's name, Amen.

Professions of Faith: Chapter 1

1. In this chapter, we discussed the definition of the words *groaning* and *confession*. Compare the two, and write down your thoughts on their differences.

_____

_____

_____

2. According to Psalm 32:3–5, what could be some of the physical and emotional consequences related to groaning?

_____

_____

_____

3. According to the Bible, what is the purpose of confessing our sin?

_____

_____

_____

4. Read Psalm 43. What does the psalmist encourage us to do while we are in the process of mourning or sadness?

_____

_____

_____

Chapter 2
The Cost of Comfort

1 In the days when the judges ruled in Israel, a severe famine came upon the land. So a man from Bethlehem in Judah left his home and went to live in the country of Moab, taking his wife and two sons with him. [2] The man's name was Elimelech, and his wife was Naomi. Their two sons were Mahlon and Kilion. They were Ephrathites from Bethlehem in the land of Judah. And when they reached Moab, they settled there.

[3] Then Elimelech died, and Naomi was left with her two sons. [4] The two sons married Moabite women. One married a woman named Orpah, and the other a woman named Ruth. But about ten years later, [5] both Mahlon and Kilion died. This left Naomi alone, without her two sons or her husband. (Ruth 1:1–5, NLT)

What's In a Name?

My husband Paul and I have four children, and when it came time to name each one, we took great interest in picking just the right moniker. We wanted strong names for each of them; we prayed, we discussed (vigorously, at times), and settled on just the perfect name for our littles because we believe that names invoke character and call out destiny. A good name is a better choice over riches (Prov. 22:1) because the person you are has eternal value. In the Bible, a name is more than a title. Many times, a name was tied to authority and power (Exod. 5:23; 1 Kgs. 21:8) and was connected to reputation (Mark 6:14; Rev. 3:1) and character (Eccles. 7:1; Matt. 6:9). When we pray or act in Jesus's name, we are stating that we are His representatives (Acts 3:16; 16:18). The power is not ours, but Jesus's working through us. There are also times when God was doing a new thing in a person that required their name to change.

All that to say, names are significant, and they play a large role not only in how we see ourselves, but also in how we respond to life.

Sticks and Stones

"Sticks and stones will break your bones but names will never hurt you!" I remember as a child hearing that rhyme on the playground and part of me really wanted to believe it. However, after such an incident of negative name calling, it was difficult to reconcile the hurt I felt and the shame experienced. I do realize for some it is easy to let those words roll off, but for others (including me), it wasn't as easy. It is particularly troublesome if a name is used consistently to describe a person or if the individual declaring those words holds a prominent place in your life. Words declared consistently become words rehearsed entirely. Not only are they fused into your psyche, but eventually they are lived out in your behavior.

On the positive side, hearing your name spoken affectionately or with promise and meaning can elevate you to purpose. This leads me to a portion of my testimony. I had been told that when I was born, my grandmother (who I called Nanny) named me. After she saw me, she proudly declared that my name would be "Lisa Dawn" for I would be the "dawning of a new day." Wow, what an awesome declaration! Unfortunately, being the serious and overly conscientious person that I am, I felt the weight of that name for many years. I perceived it to mean the whole world and its problems rested on my shoulders, and it was up to me to enlighten them in order to change their circumstances. Yes, I was a superhero of sorts, and I would bring order to the universe! It wasn't until just a few years ago, I realized my name was more of a promise fulfilled than a title of responsibility (mixed with a little ego). You see, the very month I was born represented grief to my parents, having lost a child years earlier. My birth had finally replaced the sadness that marked by that date with joy—the dawning of a new day.

Similarly, names with inherent negative meanings have proven detrimental. It may not be anything wrong with your given name, but the way in which it was spoken, a tone that communicated that you were stupid, shameful, or unworthy of time. Either way, it can have a profound effect on our future, not only how we see ourselves but also how others view us in relation to a label. The book of Ruth contains a mix of both meanings. Here are our principal characters:

>Elimelech: My God is King
>Naomi: Pleasant, delightful, and lovely
>Mahlon: Weak, sickly
>Chillion: Failing, pining
>Orpah: Fawn
>Ruth: Friend
>Boaz: Swiftness, strength

Some of those meanings are a little unfortunate. As we look into the book of Ruth, we will see how each name appears to be a little prophetic as pertaining to their outcome in the story and at times, their juxtaposition. More important than all of this is the factor of redemption because whatever you have been named, good or bad, it is in God's nature to change it into the quality He sees in you.

His Name Will Be Called

His name is Wonderful, Counselor, Mighty God, Everlasting Father, Prince of Peace, Healer, Savior, Provider, Shepherd, Messiah, Teacher, Redeemer—the list is extensive, but you get the point. The amazing thing about the names of our Lord is they aren't just titles, but pieces of His character. God is so much more intentional than we tend to be. Each label gives an opportunity for our Lord to reveal who He is. A need is exposed, and Father God has a plan and purpose waiting to be executed. When you call on the name of the Lord as Savior, you will be saved because His name backs up who He is! Names are so important that it was the first job given to Adam in the Garden of Eden (Gen. 2:19). So what happens if your name doesn't line up with God's plans?

My God Is King—Really? (Ruth 1:1–5)

What a great declaration and meaning of a name! Elimelech's name means exactly that, and yet the Bible tells us that in a season of famine, Elimelech uprooted his family and moved them to an area known for paganism and idolatry. Now before we start finger pointing, I know that many times God has not been my King, and due to fear, I have let that rule in place of His proper standing. I run all over the place, looking for a solution and reacting to a problem rather than praying and asking the Lord about it. Perhaps God intends me to endure a season that holds potential for character growth in the area of trust. How we react to a challenge reveals who is in the place of Lordship. Do we give ourselves to anxiety, or do we rest in our prayers and petitions? Are we crafting our way of escape, or are we submitting in humility to the circumstances, knowing that our Heavenly Father is more than able to give us the grace needed to walk through it?

Elimelech Chose Comfort over Obedience

Elimelech chose comfort over obedience. He settled for something that was temporary, and it ended in sorrow. While living in Moab, Elimelech died, leaving his wife Naomi and two sons, Mahlon and Chilion who chose for themselves Moabite women, Orpah and Ruth. Ten years passed, and Mahon and Chilion also died, leaving Naomi and her two daughters-in-law. Quite the train wreck, isn't it? It was a mess that I identify with all too closely. Circumstances are hard, and life is challenging. What if I just help you out a little, Lord?

I confess that I would rather live in comfort than grow in character.

The fear of the unknown can set us up to take matters into our own hands. Nobody likes to be uncomfortable in their surroundings. But we may also choose comfort over character because we have a fascination with our past. It is easy to go back to old ways: a habit that brings relief, complaining over praising, living with less when God wants to use the process to bring more. The grass is not always greener on the other side, and if it is, the cost may be too high to maintain it.

Walking through difficulty also requires discipline and an understanding of who God is.

> *And have you forgotten the encouraging words God spoke to you as his children? He said,*
>
> *"My child, don't make light of the L*ORD*'s discipline, and don't give up when he corrects you.*
> *⁶ For the L*ORD *disciplines those he loves, and he punishes each one he accepts as his child."*
>
> *⁷ As you endure this divine discipline, remember that God is treating you as his own children. Who ever heard of a*

> *child who is never disciplined by its father? ⁸ If God doesn't discipline you as he does all of his children, it means that you are illegitimate and are not really his children at all. ⁹ Since we respected our earthly fathers who disciplined us, shouldn't we submit even more to the discipline of the Father of our spirits, and live forever!*
>
> *¹⁰ For our earthly fathers disciplined us for a few years, doing the best they knew how. But God's discipline is always good for us, so that we might share in his holiness. ¹¹ No discipline is enjoyable while it is happening—it's painful! But afterward there will be a peaceful harvest of right living for those who are trained in this way."* (Heb. 12:5–11, NLT)

God's discipline yields right living, or righteousness (vs. 11). As a father, He only wants what is best for His child. As Lord, He *knows* what is best!

So what is righteousness? Righteousness is justice and grace, conformity to the revealed will of God. By submitting to His will, we can trust that His just *will* shall occur, and we *will* have the grace needed to walk in it.

> *"And do not be conformed to the patterns of this world, but be transformed by the renewing of your mind"* (Rom. 12:2 NKJV).

God's anger lasts only a moment, but His favor is for life (Ps. 30:5).

Elimelech faced the possibility of exile, exposing his family to worship false gods, estrangement from family and friends, and ultimately estrangement from God. Choosing comfort over character, we risk perpetuating crisis, and we open ourselves to the possibility of being bound again by what we may have been delivered from. We also miss out on the opportunity for God to show His strength in our situations, which would result in endurance for strength and grace for character.

We may be experiencing a season of spiritual famine, a time in our lives when we feel we have sown good seed, cultivated it, watered it, and tended to our harvest only to find it dormant. "Where are you God... did I somehow miss you"? It is in those seasons that my flesh automatically jumps to a default. How can I be comforted? Where can I be comforted? Right now I'm thinking of chocolate cake! Maybe for you, it's a place of employment where a coworker is promoted ahead of you or seems to receive favor in regardless of your performance. It could even be a past relationship that was more about the party than the process. What would it hurt to jump over there, and check it out? It would only be for a little while. Hey, it might turn into something great! Just because I'm going to dwell there doesn't mean I'm going to stay there!

> **Dwell** *(Strong's H 1481) gur: to lodge somewhere, temporarily reside, dwell as a stranger, to sojourn. From "gur" comes the noun "stranger" and "alien."*

The Hebrew behind the word *dwell* suggests a temporary stay, but we see in Ruth 1:4 that they stayed there for at least ten years. Mahlon and Chillion took Moabite women, Orpah and Ruth, to be their wives. In Deuteronomy 23:3, marriage was not prohibited with a Moabite, and the children of such a union would not be admitted into the assembly. Simplistically speaking, you can get married but won't be able to come to the family reunions.

A temporary stay lasted for ten years. Orpah and Ruth were probably exceptional women, due to the fact there is no indication Elimelech's family turned to the false gods of Moab. However, there is still a cost, and a temporary fix starts looking permanent. Circumstances aren't looking the way we'd like them to, so we settle. Recently, a dear friend was reading my book, and she sent this testimony to me. I believe it beautifully sums up my thoughts.

Am I allowing the very difficult circumstances we are walking through to keep me from God's destiny and purpose and plan for my life? Am I going to settle for less of a destiny or no destiny just because things haven't worked out the way I thought they would? Or maybe, with a new mind-set, I could envision something different—walking in my destiny despite my circumstances.

*What does this look like? I'm not sure, but it's something I'm going to be asking the Holy Spirit to help me with. I think we do settle when we feel like things aren't what we were expecting. I don't want to just go to work every day and think, this is it, this is all I'll do the rest of my life. This job I'm doing is a wonderful service for family and children, but it's not where my heart is completely. I **know** I'm supposed to be doing more. So after reading this, it challenges me to ask God to not see these difficulties as a sidetrack from my destiny, but something I'm walking through on the path to my destiny. I also am serving a purpose in these difficulties, as I serve and help my family financially. I'm not going to stop asking God for the opportunities, to even shift my full time work to the passion in my heart to write and edit and teach. He can walk me through this time, and He will help me not to settle for a lesser thing. I even feel challenged to accelerate things through my faith, just really believing and trusting God to open doors for me. It then takes me from frustration and hopelessness to excitement and purpose! I truly believe God will connect me with the right people at the right time and work out all the details. Let your favor shine on my path Lord! Let me see your goodness even in this dark time.*

> *Update: Since writing this, God placed me in a job that I love and is helping others, where I get to use my creativity, and it allows me to still have time to teach, write, and edit on my time off. I feel like I'm right where I need to be right now and that God is truly directing my path. I really see His hand moving in all this and I know it's because I asked Him to. He totally wants me to be doing what He created me to do.*

Perhaps we help God by entering into territory that ends up taking residence in our lives. "I know he's not a Christian, but he will change once we get married." Or, at first we just hear gossip, next we are listening, and finally we are participating. It's like the saying, "First you abhor, then you tolerate until you embrace it altogether."

> *Do not be unequally yoked together with unbelievers. For what fellowship has righteousness with lawlessness? And what communion has light with darkness?* [15] *And what accord has Christ with Belial? Or what part has a believer with an unbeliever?* [16] *And what agreement has the temple of God with idols? For you are the temple of the living God. As God has said: "I will dwell in them and walk among them. I will be their God, And they shall be My people."*

> [17] *Therefore*
> *"Come out from among them*
> *And be separate, says the Lord.*
> *Do not touch what is unclean,*
> *And I will receive you."*
> [18] *"I will be a Father to you,*
> *And you shall be My sons and daughters,*
> *Says the L*ORD *Almighty."*
> (2 Corinthians 6:14–18, NKJV)

God calls us to be separate from the world. He asks us to respond differently to challenges and accepts us as sons and daughters. Jesus even prays for us at great length in John 17, asking the Father to keep us through the Word. God's Word is truth and will preserve us in this world.

There is a fine line of being in the world but not being of the world. We choose our associations and what takes up residence in our lives, just like Elimelech. We may be in crisis and confusion or are experiencing a spiritual famine, but we are not alone. God is in the midst of our confusion and disappointment!

> *It was in the year King Uzziah died that I saw the Lord. He was sitting on a lofty throne, and the train of his robe filled the Temple. ² Attending him were mighty seraphim, each having six wings. With two wings they covered their faces, with two they covered their feet, and with two they flew. ³ They were calling out to each other,*
>
> *"Holy, holy, holy is the Lord of Heaven's Armies! The whole earth is filled with his glory!"*
>
> *⁴ Their voices shook the Temple to its foundations, and the entire building was filled with smoke. ⁵ Then I said, "It's all over! I am doomed, for I am a sinful man. I have filthy lips, and I live among a people with filthy lips. Yet I have seen the King, the Lord of Heaven's Armies."*
>
> *⁶ Then one of the seraphim flew to me with a burning coal he had taken from the altar with a pair of tongs. ⁷ He touched my lips with it and said, "See, this coal has touched your lips. Now your guilt is removed, and your sins are forgiven."* (Isa. 6:1–7, NLT)

This is a remarkable passage! In the midst of loss, God shows himself to Isaiah. It may even have been after a funeral. Perhaps, professional mourners would have been hired due to Uzziah's kingly status. After reading these verses one day, I wanted to dig a little deeper and decided to look up what Uzziah's name meant.

> ***Uzziah*** *(Strong's H 5818) Uzziyah: strength of Jehovah, root H5797=security.*

I believe God spoke to my heart and told me to read it this way: *"It was in the year that my **security** died that I saw the Lord."* Reading it that way brought clarity to emotions that had been surfacing due to a series of losses. Things that secured me to joy and purpose had been severed. Underneath the façade of what I presented to others, there appeared to be stability and calm, but in reality, there was chaos and uncertainty. I have an image of Linus grabbing on to his blanket, holding on so tightly that if he lost his grip, it would be a loss of something greater.

At that moment, I "lost my grip." I had to let go of my idea of what life was supposed to look like. Yet, even in my confusion and grief, I saw the Lord. The revelation of who He is lifted me out of what was. In all of His glory, He revealed areas of my life that truly needed the touch of His holiness. Impure motives were cleansed. My tongue that once spoke words of death were now purified to speak His praise. You see, what I had failed to recognize in the loss is that God is still on His throne, high and lifted up over all our dire circumstances. He still has authority and power. He continues to rule justly over the earth as I align with His kingship.

After reading this portion of my book, the Lord gave this revelation to a dear friend of mine. I am sharing it with her permission:

> *Security. The state of feeling safe, stable, and free from fear or anxiety. We often feel that our circumstances determine our security. I found through ten years of moving every*

year and even twice in two of those years, that my definition of security changed. I used to think that living in the same house, having more than enough money, and having the same friends year after year is what makes you secure.

After the first couple of years of moving, I was feeling very frustrated, I felt the Lord tell me during that very first move that I needed to just remember to be rooted and grounded in Him. It was something I had to remember and hold on to a lot! I had no idea how many times I would have to hold on to that truth.

The day my idea of security died was the day I saw how much God is my security. Giving up home ownership, giving up friends and family, to move out of state was very difficult. But God showed me that my security doesn't come from those things. My security comes from seeing God as my source, my dwelling place, my friend, my riches, and my treasure. That's where true security comes from. That is what true security is. It is dwelling in the secret place of the Most High. It is abiding in Him. And I had to change what I was seeing. I had to see the Lord as my security—not things or people. He is my security. If I have Him, I have everything.

Maybe something was yanked out of your hand. You were pulled so hard, it is difficult to distinguish where all the wounds are. It may feel that all security is taken from us by experiencing the loss of a job, friends, home, and health. The list could go on and on. However, God's desire for us is always the best. The light of His character desires to shine through in response to our circumstances, to allow His glory (the expression of His holiness) to separate us for greater works. Even when our response to heartache is nothing close to holiness, God's heart is always to draw us closer to Him. It's easy to recognize where we fall short and easier still to withdraw from a God who knows that we have. But our God is exceptional! When we are dwelling in the midst of unclean things, He will still come to us. The seraphim came and cleansed Isaiah and set Him apart for a mighty work. Note that Isaiah 6:5 sounds very much like a confession. The book of Isaiah's greatest purpose was to speak hope and promise to God's faithful remnant. It is full of the promise of restoration, redemption, and the coming of the Messiah.

Father,

I thank you for your grace that is sufficient for my every situation. I release my brokenness to You that I may be whole. I confess, that at times, I desire comfort over the character You are producing in me. I ask for strength and endurance when I walk through seasons of famine, knowing it will yield the fruit of righteousness. Thank you, Jesus, for being a great High Priest who understands what I am going through. You are worthy of all my praise!

In the precious name of Jesus, Amen.

Professions of Faith: Chapter 2

1. After reading this chapter, what might have been the cost to Elimelech and his family while residing in Moab?

_____

_____

2. What is our cost when we run back to a familiar place or habit?

_____

3. Seek the Lord and ask Him if there are any "Moab's" in your life, take time to confess your need, and give Him praise for the work He is doing in you.

_____

_____

4. Write a prayer of renewed consecration to the Lord and thank Him for His faithfulness to you.

_____

_____

Chapter 3
Rejecting Rejection

Then Naomi heard in Moab that the LORD had blessed his people in Judah by giving them good crops again. So Naomi and her daughters-in-law got ready to leave Moab to return to her homeland. ⁷ With her two daughters-in-law she set out from the place where she had been living, and they took the road that would lead them back to Judah.

⁸ But on the way, Naomi said to her two daughters-in-law, "Go back to your mothers' homes. And may the LORD reward you for your kindness to your husbands and to me. ⁹ May the LORD bless you with the security of another marriage." Then she kissed them good-bye, and they all broke down and wept.

¹⁰ "No," they said. "We want to go with you to your people."

¹¹ But Naomi replied, "Why should you go on with me? Can I still give birth to other sons who could grow up to be your husbands? ¹² No, my daughters, return to your parents' homes, for I am too old to marry again. And even if it were possible, and I were to get married tonight and bear sons, then what? ¹³ Would you wait for them to grow up and refuse to marry someone else? No, of course not, my daughters! Things are far more bitter for me than for you, because the LORD *himself has raised his fist against me."*

¹⁴ And again they wept together, and Orpah kissed her mother-in-law good-bye. But Ruth clung tightly to Naomi. ¹⁵ "Look," Naomi said to her, "your sister-in-law has gone back to her people and to her gods. You should do the same."

¹⁶ But Ruth replied, "Don't ask me to leave you and turn back. Wherever you go, I will go; wherever you live, I will live. Your people will be my people, and your God will be my God. ¹⁷ Wherever you die, I will die, and there I will be buried. May the LORD *punish me severely if I allow anything but death to separate us!" ¹⁸ When Naomi saw that Ruth was determined to go with her, she said nothing more."*

So the two of them continued on their journey. When they came to Bethlehem, the entire town was excited by their arrival. "Is it really Naomi?" the women asked.

²⁰ "Don't call me Naomi," she responded. "Instead, call me Mara, for the Almighty has made life very bitter for me. ²¹ I went away full, but the LORD *has brought me home empty. Why call me Naomi when the* LORD *has caused me to suffer and the Almighty has sent such tragedy upon me?"*

²² So Naomi returned from Moab, accompanied by her daughter-in-law Ruth, the young Moabite woman. They arrived in Bethlehem in late spring, at the beginning of the barley harvest. (Ruth 1:6–22, NLT)

Rejecting Rejection

I imagine it would be very disheartening to hear about the place you left, in order to find a better life, is now prospering and you find your family devastated by incredible loss on so many levels. In verse 6, we begin reading about Naomi and her daughters-in-law, Orpah and Ruth. Naomi hears of the harvest in Bethlehem and decides to return. Remember, she is returning to nothing. Essentially, her home and property were turned over to the "bank." Her daughters-in-law begin the journey with her, but Naomi has a compelling argument against their decision: "Even if I can have more sons, will you wait for them to be grown"? At Naomi's release, Orpah decides to return home to her family, but Ruth lovingly and willingly stays. Ruth must have seen something, through the years of relationship with Naomi. Despite the hardships, Naomi's character encourages Ruth to leave her past life and trust not in the gods of Moab, but in the one true God of Abraham, Isaac, and Jacob.

Naomi is almost unrecognizable as they enter Bethlehem. Broken and bewildered, she tells her story. Unknown to them at the time, it is a story of recovery, from loss to abundance. It is the beginning of barley harvest.

Even in her confusion over such events, Naomi still sees God in the light of His covenant. She declares to her daughters-in-law that God is kind; the connotation carries the idea of love and loyalty. God's covenant to His people is constant; it does not waver through our circumstances but is dependable and good. As she releases Orpah and Ruth, she blesses them with rest, not only for peace and the absence of struggle but also for provision and security. *"He is the LORD our God. His justice is seen throughout the land. He always stands by his covenant—the commitment he made to a thousand generations"* (Ps. 105:7–8, NLT).

It was unlikely either girl would remarry in Bethlehem due to their heritage, so returning home was to their advantage, which is what Orpah chose. However, in the Jewish culture, provision was made in the law for a woman who lost a husband in the Levirate marriage. In Ruth 1:12–13 we see a reference to it.

The Levirate Marriage, simply defined: If a married man died without children to carry on his name and inheritance, it was the unmarried brother's responsibility to marry the widow so that *"the first son she bears shall carry on the name of the dead brother so that his name will not be blotted out from Israel" (Deut. 25:6).*

The Devotion of Naomi

Ruth's witness of Naomi's devotion to God over the years must have had a profound effect on her. Ruth chose to give up her family, friends, and comfort of surroundings to embrace a new life, yet so much was unknown. Remember, aside from the harvest, there was no natural indication things would be different in Bethlehem.

This is what we know about Naomi:

1. She kept the faith in Moab (2 Tim. 4:7). I remember the transition I made as a student from Christian education into public education. I struggled at first to be faithful, but after a while, I was confronted with life outside of protected faith borders. Compromise crept in as I tried to relate to others so that I would not feel like an outsider. One of the forms of compromise came by keeping silent on issues that would require a stand, giving an impression of agreement. Eventually, I found my footing (and my Bible) and favor among believers and non-believers as I shared about my relationship with Jesus. To this day, I continue to have relationships with those I met during that time, who ask for my prayers because of my faith.

2. She believed God in the midst of adversity (2 Cor. 4:7–9). This is difficult, even for a seasoned believer, especially when there has been wave after wave of tragedy. I can't think of anything more painful than losing a child, let alone two, and your husband, too, within a short time of each other. She could have said, "I give up. I resign myself to the lifestyle and beliefs of the Moabites because God cannot be trusted. However, instead, she came home to the roots of her faith. Naomi dug deep into the

treasure of her beliefs, struck down in her emotions but not destroyed. The weights of this life pushed hard on every side, but she held it together just enough to make the trip. She may have been bewildered that her God would allow such heartache. Nevertheless, her beliefs were intact, nudging her to make the journey back to a community of faith.

3. She had a powerful influence on others (Titus 2:3–5). The fact that Orpah and Ruth began to follow Naomi out of Moab testifies to her influence on them both, and although Orpah decided to return home, Ruth affirms this truth by staying. In my mind's eye I can picture Naomi sharing her faith as she tends to her family's needs; perhaps responding in kindness to a harsh word; or as she quietly prayed to her Lord, they were watching her. Naomi's honor of life and her husband may have spoken volumes in a culture in which she didn't belong. As a family living closely to one another, nothing was missed or wasted on Ruth. Always a gleaner, she gathered the information needed to make such a life-changing decision.

She denied herself for the good of others (Phil. 2:3–4). How easy it would have been to convince Orpah and Ruth to stick around—not one, but two women to care for her needs. She could have used a myriad of guilt tactics to keep them close. Weighing the circumstances, Naomi pushed her desires aside in order for them to have fruitful lives. Her mother's heart would not allow her to be selfish; she considered others better and with her future obscured by uncertainty, tried to convince them to move on. But Ruth would have none of it!

Naomi decided to return home after ten years. Her faith, though fragile, was still intact. God's covenant to her and her people, though mired in contradiction because of her circumstances, was being rehearsed in her heart. Her example to Ruth made an impact, and Ruth stayed, following her mother-in-law into unfamiliar territory.

The Devotion of Ruth

Ruth clung to Naomi, and her commitment was not only a declaration of friendship, but also one of faith. Ruth was determined to go, which literally translated means "she made herself strong" to go with Naomi. Change, especially one of this magnitude, requires strength and determination. Defiant of the fear that could have stalled her, Ruth pressed on with Naomi.

"I confess that I look for opportunities to be rejected."

Ruth made a choice to reject rejection and took a risk. In all likelihood, living in Bethlehem as a Moabite would have solidified rejection. Instead, she pushed forward to her harvest and turned away from idolatry. So much of living in past rejection is founded in our need to change it. Although we want to reverse the cycle, without God healing our hearts, we will continue to be drawn to the familiarity of the source. Whether it be a word or an action, it cannot be swept under the rug. The demand to be heard is our mantra and justice our battle cry in order to validate our actions. Our longing to control the past needs to be released in order to give way to trust. We put our confidence in God and that He will take care of us because we are in the very palm of His hand.

BFFs

Ruth's name means "friend," according to John 15:14–16. Jesus no longer calls us servants but friends because of relationship found in the new covenant. As friends of God, we now have the opportunity to know what the Father is saying and we have the ability to partner with Him. These are no longer the days of relying on the prophet to speak the heart of God to His people; we have access through Jesus the Waymaker. He knows better than anyone what it feels like to be rejected. Isaiah 53 prophetically paints a very pointed picture of what Jesus would experience.

Jesus was despised, rejected, full of sorrow, and acquainted with grief. He more than shook hands with sadness; he wore it as a garment that we would trade as praise. The emotional beating Jesus took was just as heinous as the physical one He endured. It goes on to say, "like one from whom men hide their faces He was despised, and we did not appreciate His worth or esteem Him"(vs. 3, AMP).

As I type this, I am overwhelmed at how superficial I can be. I am thinking of the unlovely of society and the many times I have turned away my eyes from their plight, uncomfortable by their appearance or concerned of what I may be required by a loving God to show them His love. You see, I have personally found that rejection does not have to be overt to wound. It can be as simple as seeing someone you know and making an effort to engage, if only with a smile, and have that person quickly look away.

We would be a mess if everyone who didn't smile at us caused us offense. A few years back, my husband and I, along with some friends, took a trip to Philadelphia. While sightseeing, as we came upon an area, we heard some music. It was getting dark, and I have to confess, I felt a little uncomfortable. But as we ventured closer, we saw that it was coming from someone who could be easily forgotten from society, with tattered clothes, messy, and a little smelly. We lingered a few minutes and as we conversed with our friends, each of us felt that the Lord wanted to minister to this talented man. We engaged in some conversation, and as he told us his story of mistakes, challenges, and hurt, we learned that years earlier he had served in a church, but life and choices took him on a different road.

We sang with him, shared the encouragement that the Lord impressed on our minds, and prayed for a revelation of the love of God to come to his heart. As much as we wanted to be a blessing to him, through our experience, we were blessed. Had we not taken the time and listened to Holy Spirit, it would have been just another spot on our trip. I'm a little disappointed with myself to admit that there have been far too many times I have just walked away from a situation like this. Looking forward, with blinders on, as if to say, "nothing to see here." I'm talking about times of brokenness in a person's life that require some care from us, a recognition that their life matters, that, by a simple gesture like a smile or a word of greeting, can validate their existence. I have prayed for him over the years, since that trip, that the words we spoke awakened his heart to re-dedication to the Lord.

It is also apparent to me how close I have come to living in a similar place. But for God, it is even more amazing to me that the King of the universe understands our frailty to the point that at every level, Jesus, God's own son, paid the price on the Cross. *He experienced rejection so we wouldn't have to **live in it** and supplied the grace for us to **extend it to others.*** Father God doesn't look away; He sees His creation—His child. Ruth not only shook off rejection, she exemplified her name and was a friend.

Abraham was one of a few to be called a friend in the Old Covenant because he believed God and trusted that what God said would come to pass (James 2:23). Abraham was old. Sarah was old. There were many years of natural life that could have resulted in fruitfulness though it didn't happen, and yet, Abraham still believed that God would fulfill His promise.

Perhaps, in the middle of her crisis, Naomi, spoke out of grief and confusion. She announced to her friends that she would rather be called "Mara" or bitter, which is a sharp contrast from what her name really means: "Pleasant or lovely." When we are hurting, it is easy to speak from that which encourages isolation rather than a place of faith. Abraham also faltered in that he chose to take matters into own hands with Hagar, and yet God in His goodness credited Abraham's faith as righteous and even spoke promise over the offspring, Ishmael. Little does Naomi know, God had begun the great set-up. Speaking or acting out of frustration may bring consequences; still, God will do a great work on our behalf despite our humanity! However, we can set a watch over our mouths so we can declare God's promises while waiting for unfinished providence, especially considering life and death are in the power of the tongue (Prov. 18:21). Easier said than done, right?

Shame on You!

I have always struggled with that phrase even before I fully understood what it meant. Why would we want to speak that over someone let alone our children or loved ones? Didn't Jesus die to remove it from our lives (1 Pet. 2:6–7)? Shame is also the result of horrible abuses perpetrated on us by individuals, in most cases, we have trusted. In those situations, prayers of deliverance and a Spirit-led counselor may be needed to help untangle the lies of Satan.

I have yet to know someone who has lived a perfect life despite my best efforts to present mine as an offering (insert eye roll here). Mistakes, missteps, sin—however you want to label it—all result in the feeling of unworthiness. Each one of us has missed the mark; all have fallen short of God's glory (Rom. 3:23). When we are convicted of sin, oftentimes we feel guilty and recognize what we have done is bad. Shame is different in that it is closely tied to our identity. We not only know what we have done, or others to us, is wrong, we now associate it with who we are. *We are wrong, bad, or misfits.* Shame shapes our beliefs until what is left is a disfigured representation of who we really are.

Shame is an enemy of trust. It causes one to question what and who is reliable by using disappointment and regret, especially when we have been victimized. Our enemy, Satan, loves shame as it hinders God's people from living an abundant, faith-filled life. Shame operates in control, holding captive the life that has believed its report. It should come as no surprise how the word *ashamed* in the Bible is defined.

The Hebrew word for *ashamed* is: *buwsh* (H 954), and it means to be delayed, disappointed, confused; to become dry.

If the enemy can keep your experiences cloaked in regret, we will never move into the promises God has for each of us.

Delayed

It is compounded when we have believed for something, stepped out, and failed. I have been there, and in my limited human understanding have walked into life, trusting God to move a certain way, only to learn His ways really *are* higher. Perhaps you've experienced something similar. The work you are called to ended up becoming your identity. If *it* failed, I have failed, or worse, I believe that I am a failure. For me, I don't want to talk about it because it can be embarrassing to admit I wasn't right. Or, maybe like Abraham, the timing isn't right.

The delay may not mean *no* but an opportunity for growth, as our plans become refined. Our microwave perspective of life confines our faith to human reasoning, allowing the enemy—flesh or spiritual—to exploit our disappointment. As brothers and sisters in Christ, we aren't always the most supportive in these times. We may pat each other on the head as if to minimize what we don't understand or what may be challenging for us to lay hold of regarding their promise. When this happens, it can become a prime opportunity for shame to be joined with rejection. We may be looking for the approval of man instead of receiving the acceptance of our Savior, Jesus Christ.

If it is a God-given dream and He has given the strategy to work it out, no delay will keep it from coming to pass. A delay may be working out the details and not turning down the idea. Sometimes what looks like rejection is actually God protecting us from circumstances that would potentially bring us harm or lead us away from His plan. The shame we feel might be embarrassment or even pride. Daily surrender to the Lord, keep your eyes focused on Him, and allow your plans to unfold in His timing. Either way, if we are not careful (or prayerful), we may forfeit the prize before we have even started, even though what is communicated may cause one to think twice about living boldly.

Disappointed and Confused

> [21] *And there by the Ahava Canal, I gave orders for all of us to fast and humble ourselves before our God. We prayed that he would give us a safe journey and protect us, our children, and our goods as we traveled.* [22] *For I was ashamed to ask the king for soldiers and horsemen[1] to accompany us and protect us from enemies along the way. After all, we had told the king, "Our God's hand of protection is on all who worship him, but his fierce anger rages against those who abandon him."[23] So we fasted and earnestly prayed that our God would take care of us, and he heard our prayer.* (Ezra 8:21–2, 3, NLT)

In this passage, we see Ezra's faith to lead Israel to Jerusalem, fulfilling what had been prophesied. He had heard about what God would do, but it was his trust that would cause him to entreat God instead of the hand of a gracious king. He called upon the people to fast and pray; a wonderful model for those times when we are convicted to move in a courageous fashion. They asked for:

1. Guidance—We may have a word of prophecy or a promise, but it is in our best interest to not blindly move out without the Spirit of God to guide us through His Word and counsel from other faith-filled leaders.

2. Assistance—No one is an island, and God never intended us to do things solely on our own. Not only did God provide supernaturally for the rebuilding of the temple, but He also provided the workers and protection for follow through. In the New Testament, the birth of the church was not in a building but in people beginning, with Peter's revelation of Christ (Matt. 16:13–19). We become the body of Christ and continue to work together (Eph. 4:16).

3. Authenticity—Ezra had the favor of the king, but he had been testifying of God's goodness and would have been *ashamed* to ask anything of man that he had been declaring about God (Ezra 8:22). He didn't want to undermine God's power and name, so he sought Him through prayer and fasting.

Dry Seasons

One of the interesting parts of the definition of shame is "to become dry." I can't speak for you, but I have had a few seasons where I felt like the life was sucked out of me. I was hit so hard by circumstances that it took a minute (by minute, I mean months) to catch my breath. Just when I thought things would turn back to normal, I was expending strength to resolve another issue. I have found that in those times of fighting the fight, keeping the faith can leave you depleted and weary. At the root may even be a feeling of humiliation—that we can't live up to the victorious Christian walk. If we get stuck there, we become dry. We may even be tempted to give up, wondering if it really is worth the fight. God loves us and is not going to leave us walking in shame and will give us the power to keep from stepping back into it with our choices.

> *You shall eat in plenty and be satisfied,*
> *and praise the name of the* LORD *your God,*
> *who has dealt wondrously with you.*
> *And my people shall never again be put to shame.*
> *[27] You shall know that I am in the midst of Israel,*
> *and that I am the* LORD *your God and there is none else.*
> *And my people shall never again be put to shame.*
> (Joel 2:26–27, NKJV)

Call on the Lord; lean into Him. He is in the midst of even our most dire trials. Take time and read the whole chapter of Joel 2. The complete chapter is summed up in regard to refreshing.

Choices made long ago had left Naomi confused and broken by her bitter circumstances. But she was moving in the right direction: back to Bethlehem and covenant. She was empty but soon would be filled, for it was the beginning of barley harvest.

Father,

Forgive me when I choose to return to the past and rejection. I receive that You, Jesus, bore rejection so that I could be accepted. I walk away from my spiritual and emotional Moab, moving forward with ordered steps to my place of harvest. You have already begun a work to rebuild my spiritual lineage, and you are faithful to complete it. Thank you for your provision and grace.

In Jesus's name, Amen.

Professions of Faith: Chapter 3

1. What are some ways Ruth may have experienced rejection or discrimination?

_____

_____

2. Naomi was a strong example to Ruth; in what ways does her life speak to us today?

_____

_____

3. Ruth was determined to go with Naomi; in other words, she "made herself strong" to go. Have you ever walked through a season when you made a choice to be strong? Was there a scripture that kept you going?

_____

_____

4. Read Psalm 71 and note the different scenarios the psalmist wrote about while praising God in his circumstances.

_____

_____

Chapter 4
Following Favor or Estrangement Entanglement

2 Now there was a wealthy and influential man in Bethlehem named Boaz, who was a relative of Naomi's husband, Elimelech.

² One day Ruth the Moabite said to Naomi, "Let me go out into the harvest fields to pick up the stalks of grain left behind by anyone who is kind enough to let me do it."

Naomi replied, "All right, my daughter, go ahead." ³ So Ruth went out to gather grain behind the harvesters. And as it happened, she found herself working in a field that belonged to Boaz, the relative of her father-in-law, Elimelech. (Ruth 2:1–3, NLT)

After twenty years at home as a mommy and co-leader in ministry with my husband, we found ourselves needing extra income. Boldly (and fearfully), I found a job at a retail shop in the mall. I remember driving there and thinking, *What am I doing?* Anxiety gripped me, but I was determined to follow through and help with the provision for our growing family. I would rehearse through tears, "I am strong and courageous; God is with me wherever I go." What I lacked in experience, I would make up in excellence of heart. After a few months of stressful experiences with customers, a couple register mess-ups, and setting aside the guilt of leaving my children home at night, the Lord led me to an administrative position during the day when my kids would not miss me.

I was grateful for the job change, and I believe that by stepping out into the first retail position, God honored me with the second. Although Ruth did not need to care for little ones, she needed a means to provide. She sought permission from Naomi to glean in the fields. Ruth was not looking for the easy way out but was bravely seeking favor. I can identify so much with that situation. As much as I wanted to stay home, I knew God would help me if I stepped out in faith, and the field I "happened" upon was filled with grace. Actually, that wasn't the name of my employer, but it may as well have been because I was hired for the position with little in the way of a skill set. God gave me a spiritual Boaz. I gleaned daily with women who had more education and greater abilities than me. It was humbling at times, not only due to my lack of expertise, but for the kindness and patience I was so generously afforded, especially during the early days of my position. I can imagine it was humbling for Ruth in different ways, bending down to pick up what was left over as harvesters retrieved the best grain. Gleaning was hard work, but she was diligent to persevere. This selfless act led her to the field of Boaz and prepared the way for redemption.

All in the Family

Who was Boaz anyway? We know that he was related to Naomi through the lineage of her husband Elimelech. His name means "by strength." Boaz was likely very respected, as tradition holds that Boaz was a mighty warrior. As a landowner, we are told that Boaz was a man of means, and the Hebrew here implies more than just economic prosperity. He was a man rich in character, and his name reflects power and social standing within the community. He was filled with compassion and respect for the law by allowing his fields to be gleaned.

Gleaning: *Under the law (Lev. 19:9), generous treatment was provided to the poor at harvest time. In reaping, the corners were left by the owners for gleaning. The owner was not to reap to the extreme edge, nor gather together the ears left on the field. In the vineyard and olive plantations the fallen fruit was to be left for the distressed and foreigner (Deut. 24:20–22).*

Honor Thy Mother (in-Law)

I am incredibly blessed to not only have a virtuous mother, but also a mother-in-law who embodies excellence, both women surpassing the value of rubies. In the story of Ruth (2:2), we see an incredible amount of honor Ruth that bestowed on Naomi. She was acting with dignity and purpose to not only care for herself, but also her mother-in-law. Ruth could have made the assumption that Naomi would glean with her, but she took the initiative to go by herself, and by asking for permission, she is communicating that there is no expectation for Naomi to work in the fields. Ruth is making it clear that Naomi may rest, not only physically but also emotionally from trying to figure out where their next meal would come from. I have been in situations where it was enough that I pulled myself out of bed in the morning. The "Ruths" in my life took care of me, speaking encouragement, offering assistance by cleaning my home or making a meal, and even using humor to diffuse a troubling time with laughter. They were acting, or better yet, *being* the true friend I needed by sticking close to my field of adversity.

Ruth acted with a meek spirit, which is considerate, unassuming, gentle, and mild. When we have a spirit of meekness, we yield our rights to others, and we walk in the courage needed to let God call all the shots. We don't have to take the reins and guide our future. I've heard meekness described as "power under control." What does that mean exactly? In the Bible, meekness is a character trait that implies the ability to defer to others while exercising an inward strength, especially resigning one's circumstances to God as He directs the outcome. Meekness, oftentimes, is seen by our culture today as a weakness, which is why it is so often translated as "gentleness," but in ancient cultures it was revered as being a trait of noblemen and kings. The result of such compliance is explained as "the patient and hopeful endurance of undesirable circumstances identifies the person as externally vulnerable and weak, but inwardly resilient and strong," which is why the Bible admonishes us in this way:

> *Blessed are the meek for they shall inherit the earth.* (Matt. 5:5, NKJV)

> *But the meek shall inherit the earth, and shall delight themselves in the abundance of peace.* (Ps. 37:11, NKJV)

Meekness is not weakness as we see in the life of Jesus (Matt. 11:29; 21:5); He always submitted to the Father, doing what God said and not what He wanted. Submitting to the will of the Father was paramount in fulfilling God's plan of redemption.

Bumper Crops or Bumpy Crops?

"But the fruit of the Spirit is love, joy, peace, patience, kindness, goodness, faithfulness, gentleness (meekness) and self-control" (Gal. 5:22, NKJV). Fruit is not a gift; it must be planted and cultivated. It comes with discipline by clearing out the rocks and preparing the soil for seed. Then after the planting, one must tend to the field by watering and keeping pests and weeds from destroying the tender shoots that break through the soil. Finally, when the plants are mature, you must know the right time to harvest. The crop, if picked too early, will yield fruit that is hard and lacking in flavor. Our lives can mirror this analogy.

Without the work of the Spirit of God and our humility to submit to Him, it is too easy to take matters into our hands, settling for a heart condition that is uneven with issues and making it difficult for any seed of the Word to penetrate and produce life. Or, if we have allowed a divine work, we become impatient and decide it is time for others to partake in our gifts. Not only is it unpleasant, like eating an unripe peach, but we may come off as callous or hard; unseasoned by the lack of maturity that being sensitive to the Spirit would bring. We may feel that we're ready, but yielding and inquiring of the Lord will confirm and make a way for us.

In humility, Ruth put her feelings aside for the well-being of Naomi, and her character led her choices. She did not react rebelliously to her condition in life, but she was controlled and dignified. Her example and obedience was yielding a bumper crop of good deeds.

> *[13] If you are wise and understand God's ways, prove it by living an honorable life, doing good works with the humility that comes from wisdom. [14] But if you are bitterly jealous and there is selfish ambition in your heart, don't cover up the truth with boasting and lying. [15] For jealousy and selfishness are not God's kind of wisdom. Such things are earthly, unspiritual, and demonic. [16] For wherever there is jealousy and selfish ambition, there you will find disorder and evil of every kind.*
>
> *[17] But the wisdom from above is first of all pure. It is also peace loving, gentle at all times, and willing to yield to others. It is full of mercy and the fruit of good deeds. It shows no favoritism and is always sincere. [18] And those who are peacemakers will plant seeds of peace and reap a harvest of righteousness.* (James 3:13–18, NLT)

Godly character is the result of godly wisdom. Ruth chose the path of wisdom and not the path of entitlement. Her expectation was not in that she would be granted provision. Instead she sought after the favor of gracious landowners, revealing to us a beautiful picture of salvation. When we come to an end of ourselves, it is the grace and goodness of

God that draws us to seeking His way (Rom. 2:4). Through Jesus Christ, we have been given a new path to walk, new territory to pursue, and a life to be lived in abundance!

Everything in Ruth's life could have been met with condemnation, a sentence spoken over her simply by her heritage. Even now, I am reflecting on the possible legacy that would have remained had Jesus not pulled me out of the pit. Although I accepted the Lord into my heart at a young age, that did not spare me from developing an unhealthy mind-set. Thought patterns would lead to decisions and decisions to unhealthy structures. Eventually, those unstable structures would need to be torn down and replaced, finally rebuilding upon the rock, Christ Jesus. We can continue feeling judged, not necessarily by others, but by our own contempt bound by failure. Or, we can receive His grace.

It is easy to believe the lie that no one else has been through what we have, that we are somehow odd and different just by observing our spheres of influence. Some of us (myself included) are really good at keeping it all together for onlookers. We frame our world like a beautiful piece of art, only to realize later that it is a piece of forgery, snared by the desire to share something of worth. We become entangled by either believing we are of no value due to our experience or presenting a picture that life has been lived in perfection, both of which deny the grace of God.

Ruth could have chosen a path of estrangement; embracing the differences that seemed to herald her existence and forgetting her initial declaration of faith to Naomi.

The word *estrangement* (H2114) in Hebrew means to be "treated as a foreigner, turned away, seen as profane."

> **"I confess that at times I feel alone in my circumstances and estranged from others."**

The enemy would like nothing better than for God's children to feel estranged. If Satan can get us to believe that no one else has gone through what we are going through, he has snared us. Our desire to belong then results in justification. Even if our trials have resulted from no cause of our own, the need to know why will fuel a reason to justify our self-righteousness. Job faced this same dilemma when he said, "Though I justify myself my own mouth would condemn me" (Job 9:20, KJV). In all of our justifications in life, we can't make it right, and we run the risk of developing a judgmental spirit. It is interesting to note that one of the root words for *justify* is "vengeance." *"For if you are trying to make yourselves right with God by keeping the law, you have been cut off from Christ! You have fallen away from God's grace"* (Gal. 5:4, NLT).

We can become estranged from Christ when we attempt to be justified by the law by letting our conditions provoke us to shrink back and live in lack, believing this is the way it is. The better choice is to seek after the one who brings favor.

Remember Joseph? He was a young man loved by his father, spurned by his brothers due to jealousy, and gifted by God as a dreamer and visionary (his story can be found in Gen. 37–48). Unfortunately his overconfident attitude or arrogance left a bad taste in the mouths of his brothers as he bragged concerning his dreams of superiority. In their anger, they first thought to kill him, but instead sold him to merchants passing by their flocks as they camped. God used years of trial and seclusion to temper and build character in Joseph in order to fulfill a mighty plan that God had purposed early on in Joseph's life. Most of what he endured was unfair as he experienced one disappointment after another; hopeful expectations were lost to false accusations that led to broken promises.

Joseph remained faithful and kept his integrity amidst trying circumstances because he believed that God could be trusted. An immature response to his God-dreams enslaved him, but eventually, it was because of a dream that Joseph was elevated out of the pit and into the palace, thus saving his captors along with the people of his heritage. It was because of lack that his brothers sought him for help, not knowing who he was. You see, when we allow God to work in hearts,

He will transform us so beautifully that we will be unrecognizable by those in our past. When we were once a worm, unattractive and raw, we can be changed into a beautiful butterfly, released to soar above our storms. Then, Joseph does something extraordinary; instead of punishing his brothers, he reveals his identity and brings them along with his father into a fruitful place of blessing. Joseph declares with substance the results of the grace worked in him.

> *⁵ But don't be upset, and don't be angry with yourselves for selling me to this place. It was God who sent me here ahead of you to preserve your lives. ⁶ This famine that has ravaged the land for two years will last five more years, and there will be neither plowing nor harvesting. ⁷ God has sent me ahead of you to keep you and your families alive and to preserve many survivors.* (Gen. 45:5–7, NLT)

God used Joseph but not until after He remade him. God had to work humility into his frame, grace in his countenance, and integrity in his stature. Many lives were saved because of the journey Joseph reluctantly walked.

Loss of any kind, disappointment, betrayal, unfair treatment, and being misunderstood does not always make sense. In fact, it rarely does. But when it is yielded to a good and wise heavenly Father, it will turn from ashes to beauty. One must only seek it out.

Hide and Seek

God's favor not only has led us to salvation, it leads us to divine appointments. Ruth "happened" to come to the field belonging to Boaz. What are the chances Ruth would come to that field? It would be interesting to know the statistical probability involved in that. As a follower of Jesus, life does not consist of random possibilities, chance encounters, or happenstance. We can align our hearts to trust, knowing that

He will work it out for good—because He is good! Our circumstances may be undesirable, but if we keep walking, at some point we will meet up with purpose.

"We may throw the dice, but the Lord determines how they fall" (Prov. 16:33, NLT). Be careful not to make light of encounters, casual conversations, and accidental meetings, for they may change the very course of your life. Consider these facts:

- An apple falling to the ground suggested to Isaac Newton that there was more to God's creation and unlocked the mystery of gravity.

- When James Watt lifted the lid of a tea kettle it led to the invention of the steam engine.

- A trust and faith in God prompts a young mother to release her son into the crocodile-infested Nile River, and he was discovered by a princess to be raised up and anointed by God to be a deliverer.

The Currency of Mercy

In our despair, God will lead. In our hopeless state, we are not alone. Surrendering to Jesus, His plans cannot be thwarted. As our Redeemer, He is always looking for ways to reach back and reset our future. In our grief, we may not see it in that moment, but if we can hold fast to the Word of God, we might just witness a redemptive miracle.

My husband, Paul, is not only a staff pastor but a managing funeral director for the outreach funeral home ministry of our church. As God has graced him, he ministers to people in various circumstances; sometimes the situation is especially tragic. One such time involved a family who lost their beautiful young adult daughter to a terrible accident. They planned the service to honor their cherished daughter. Many people came to pay their respects. Among the attendees was a friend of hers, I'll call Teresa, who came to the service. Time passed, and to the surprise of the family, they heard from Teresa. She shared how on the exact same day of the memorial, she was scheduled for an abortion but decided to cancel and attend the service instead.

Teresa was so moved by the testimony of the life of her friend, that she rededicated her life to Jesus and decided against having the abortion all together. Months passed and she gave birth to a beautiful baby girl, choosing to memorialize her friend by naming her baby after her. Of course, this doesn't make everything all better, but it brought tremendous healing and comfort. God's mercy was not only extended to Teresa but became an overflow of comfort to their broken hearts. Although their daughter is with Jesus, her friend, Teresa, came back to life through faith. Teresa's baby will not only live, but will be raised to declare the glory of God. Isn't that beautiful?

Later on, in a couple chapters, we will see in detail how complete the word *redemption* is for each of us. It is a holy exchange: letting go of our grief and disappointments on one side to pick up faith on another, much like gleaning. Ruth let go of her past to lay hold of her future. I'm sure it wasn't easy, just like for many of us, but if we can fix our eyes on Jesus, we will find something of greater value on the other side.

> Father God,
>
> I confess to You any desire to justify the disappointments in my life. I choose to be meek and follow after favor, seeking wisdom above all else. I trust Your plan, knowing You have only good for me, full of hope and a future. I declare that I am not alone; You are with me and will lead me in paths of righteousness, dripping with abundance.
>
> In Jesus's precious name, Amen.

Professions of Faith: Chapter 4

1. Ruth showed us in chapter 2 how to show honor to others. According to 1 Corinthians 12:20–27, how do we show honor to fellow believers?

_____

_____

2. In this chapter we discussed meekness; what does it mean to you? (Matt. 5:5; 11:29; 21:5; Num. 12:3)

_____

_____

3. Read James 3:13–18. According to this passage, when is there confusion? What type of actions result in wisdom?

_____

_____

4. After prayer and reflection, has there ever been a time when you allowed your circumstances to lead you to feeling estranged in your relationship to God or His people? If so, how did you walk out of it?

_____

_____

Chapter 5
From Preparation to Provision

*⁴ While she was there, Boaz arrived from Bethlehem and greeted the harvesters. "The L*ORD *be with you!" he said.*

*"The L*ORD *bless you!" the harvesters replied.*

⁵ Then Boaz asked his foreman, "Who is that young woman over there? Who does she belong to?"

⁶ And the foreman replied, "She is the young woman from Moab who came back with Naomi. ⁷ She asked me this morning if she could gather grain behind the harvesters. She has been hard at work ever since, except for a few minutes' rest in the shelter."

⁸ Boaz went over and said to Ruth, "Listen, my daughter. Stay right here with us when you gather grain; don't go to any other fields. Stay right behind the young women working in my field. ⁹ See which part of the field they are harvesting, and then follow them. I have warned the young men not to treat you roughly. And when you are thirsty, help yourself to the water they have drawn from the well."

[10] Ruth fell at his feet and thanked him warmly. "What have I done to deserve such kindness?" she asked. "I am only a foreigner."

*[11] "Yes, I know," Boaz replied. "But I also know about everything you have done for your mother-in-law since the death of your husband. I have heard how you left your father and mother and your own land to live here among complete strangers. [12] May the L*ORD*, the God of Israel, under whose wings you have come to take refuge, reward you fully for what you have done."*

[13] "I hope I continue to please you, sir," she replied. "You have comforted me by speaking so kindly to me, even though I am not one of your workers." (Ruth 2:4–13, NLT)

Over thirty years ago, I went to visit a church of my heritage. I had heard of special meetings that were occurring and decided to check them out. I needed a little refreshing in my spirit, and it would give me a chance to fellowship with some friends who were dear to my heart. Little did I know that decision set me up to meet my future husband. I found out later that as I was attending these services, my husband (an acquaintance then) was asking about me—who I was, my family, and my relationship with the Lord. I assume I received a good report because here we are thirty-four years later, with four children and five grandchildren, joys and triumphs and countless experiences. Our marriage is intact and thriving, our love deeper than ever!

I can see Boaz inquiring about Ruth in my mind's eye. He was impressed by her work ethic and treatment of her mother-in-law Naomi, so much so that he bestows favor on her through the process of providing food and arranging protection from harm while gleaning. Ruth is clearly humbled by his kindness toward her and reminds Boaz of her nationality, maybe to protect herself from ridicule if it should come up later. But he only recognizes the covering and humility that Ruth has decided to submit to. As she is gleaning, it appears that Ruth would almost disappear; becoming assimilated into her work. She is not positioning herself to be seen, drawing attention to her industriousness, or even inquiring about the owner of the field she is tending. She is simply serving, doing whatever it takes to provide. On the other hand, gleaning was twofold; it met the needs of the gleaner and cleared the land for the owner, and in some sense preparing it for the next crop.

My confession: I struggle with preparation.

Have you ever found yourself in a season that wherever you turned in the physical, you were literally moving forward, but in the area of your purpose or calling, it seemed you were going backwards? Every step uncovered flaws, attitudes, unbelief, fear, or pride, each being exposed, like stones needing to be removed before the crop can present itself. You've planted seed, watered it with prayer and even tears, and just when you think it's harvest time, things come to a screeching halt! It's confusing, frustrating, and disheartening. But, loved ones, it is also necessary.

Preparation of the Soil

The Bible has much to say about preparation; in this next section we will take a look at the practical side.

- Portions of the land were marked off and divided for the various products of the soil (Isa. 28:25). It was protected from wild animals by ledges and walls (Isa. 5:5; Num. 22:24).

- The compost was prepared from straw trodden in the waste (Isa. 25:10). It consisted from elements of animal remains as a combination to enrich the soil.

- The land was also burned to destroy weeds and any noxious herbs. This process was used to supplement to the soil.

- The soil was then plowed, cleared of any stones, and dirt clods were broken up (Isa. 28:24).

Now I realize some of that is pretty descriptive, but hopefully not nauseating for those who are sensitive. There are graphic pictures in scripture that I believe speak to us prophetically and can be seen in a practical way, especially in the Old Testament.

In verse 4 of Ruth 2, we read an exchange between Boaz and his workers: "The Lord be with you" and "The Lord bless you." This suggests that even in the time of the judges, there were still people who glorified God in their daily lives.

In our world today, we live with similar struggles. People deny God's power or that He even exists, cursing is common, self-reliance and selfishness team up, making a need for God futile. Our nation seems to be under judgment or at least reaping some heavy consequences. So here we are, perhaps we feel small, but what does God say to us—His reapers? "The Lord is with you!" *"But you belong to God, my dear children. You have already won a victory over those people, because the Spirit who lives in you is greater than the spirit who lives in the world"* (1 John 4:4, NLT).

We are not alone! As believers, the Spirit of God lives in us, and the victory Jesus apprehended for us, is ours as well. However, there is groundwork needed in every child of God to fulfill a finished work. The victory may be ours to grasp, but the training is not lost to the prize.

There is a lesson for us in the soil:

- The land divided: The Lord has called us out of darkness into light to proclaim His praise. He made us a special people, distinct and chosen (1 Pet. 2:9).

- Enrichment of the soil: The blood of Jesus enriches our lives, sanctifying and calling us to obedience (1 Pet. 1:2).

- Fire in the soil: The refiner's fire comes to destroy all that could entangle and choke us. The result of the fire proves us genuine, and enriches those around us giving praise to Jesus (Isa. 10:17; 1 Pet. 1:7).

- ⚘ Break up the fallow ground. Through brokenness Jesus gives us hearts of flesh so that seeds of righteousness may be sown (Hos. 10:12; Ezek. 36:26).

Fighting Fire with Fire

In August of 1949, a wildfire in Mann Gulch on Helena National Forest in Montana proved to be disastrous to a group of smokejumpers called in to fight this horrific blaze. Robert Wagner "Wag" Dodge was the foreman in charge of this crew of fifteen men. Shortly after they were air-dropped into the area, the flames proved more aggressive than what they had anticipated. As a wall of fire pursued them, it was clear to Wag that their situation was dire; they would not be able to outrun the blaze that put all their lives in jeopardy. To the confusion of his team, he took a match and threw it on the grass, and flames quickly began to surround the area. He instructed his men to do the same and get in the middle and lay down. As the fire consumed the land around them, this act preserved Wag's life. Sadly, most of the men ran to find protection and did not follow his lead, perishing in the fire.

How many times when we are walking in the fire, and instead of surrendering to the process, we fight it? Perhaps we think we might outrun flames, so we run, but circumstances have outpaced us. How could a good God allow us to endure such heated circumstances?

"I have refined you, but not as silver is refined. Rather, I have refined you in the furnace of suffering" (Isa. 48:1, NLT). Possibly, He allows the circumstance because we belong to Him and the most precious thing is *us*. All that is around us that is not usable must be discarded, burned off, and even destroyed for the sake of His name or His name's sake—you and me!

I will rescue you for my sake—
yes, for my own sake!
I will not let my reputation be tarnished,

and I will not share my glory with idols! (Isa. 48:11, NLT)

The Message Bible states it this way:

> *I've refined you, but not without fire.*
> *I've tested you like silver in the furnace of affliction.*
> *Out of myself, simply because of who I am, I do what I do.*
> *I have my reputation to keep up.*
> *I'm not playing second fiddle to either gods or people.*
> (Isa. 48:10–11, MSG)

No one enjoys suffering or to be afflicted with hardship. Well, I don't anyway, and I will do whatever it takes to be far from it. Unfortunately, it doesn't work that way. We are loved too greatly to be left to our own devices. God disciplines those He loves (Heb. 12:5–6) and receives us as His children. Therefore, we won't be kept from it, *but* we will be kept in it. God is God, and He will not allow us to be equated with His glory, but He will allow us to partner with it, and the fire purifies our motivations so that He will be exalted. Correction leads to deliverance, bringing revision and perfection. The Lord doesn't necessarily bring on our trials, but He will use them, just the same, to expose areas that need to look a little more like Him.

Silencing the Tormentor

Community is important and necessary for developing character and sharpening gifts. As we serve alongside our brothers and sisters, there is opportunity for what is under the surface to reveal itself, and if we are not careful, we will find ourselves tripping over our pride. It can happen when we are working toward a goal and the task becomes challenging. Insecurity and lack of forgiveness are breeding grounds to become discouraged and discontented in the process, as we feed thoughts full of resentment, hopelessness, and inequality. Eventually, these beliefs loom up and become so distorted they change from a fleeting thought to outright torment and sin.

The refiner's fire also rids us of the tormentor. The name of *Beelzebub* means "lord of the flies or lord of the dwelling." Just like a fly, the enemy comes back to torment those places in us that are dead, impure, or stagnant. The Lord showed me in my own life that when we are operating in unforgiveness, living in the past, licking our wounds, or even justifying impurity, it is an opportunity for the enemy of the house to come and torment me.

As individuals, in Christ we contain the very presence of God (John 17:23), the dwelling place of His Spirit. To be rid of the enemy, Beelzebub, we must repent and allow Holy Spirit as the all-consuming fire to burn away all trash talk, whether spoken out loud or an internal dialogue.

As a community, we facilitate a place of torment by holding within ourselves hurts and offenses. We are called not to live as individuals but to become living stones (Eph. 2:19–22; 1 Pet. 2:5) that make up a spiritual house. How we live and treat each other determines who the lord of the dwelling is. Conflict will come and sparks will fly as "iron sharpens iron" (Prov. 27:17). What is important is that things are being built, shaped, or reinforced, not torn apart and destroyed. Unfortunately as humans, our flesh can get in the way. We may have thoughts that our way, opinions, or experience is better than someone else's—even those of the leadership. And you know what? They might be—but that is up to the Lord to position you in an orderly manner. If we are not surrendering to the purifying fire of discipline, our good intentions can turn into rotten attitudes, undermining the very foundation you desire to build. The only way to be rid of the lingering effects of a dung hill is by fire. Fire either purifies or destroys (Mal. 3:3; Matt. 3:11). If we repent and walk in love, we will be purified and established (Eph. 3). If we allow the hurts and offenses to linger, they will eventually destroy us. It may be one of the reasons the apostles were told to "shake the dust from their feet" in Matthew 10:14 and Acts 13:51. Jesus was telling them to release the rejection they experience when declaring His kingdom and let go of anything that would make them unclean. They are rejecting the message, not the messenger.

Father God desires a field pliable enough to be able to harvest in, one that is void of rocks and clods so that when the seed is planted, it takes root. He wants a field fertile for His Spirit and His Word to germinate a bountiful harvest. Where we are deficient, He wants to fill us. God works in our lack to prove what a generous Father He is! As our hearts receive truth, we also receive courage to embrace provision in a way different from our expectations.

During the preparation, our gracious Heavenly Father is planning to provide for us.

What's in the Fridge?

I have never really enjoyed leftovers, which might have to do with how particular I am about food (some might even say picky). Of course, leftovers are of extreme benefit during a week filled with challenges brought by work, school, sports, or even a crisis. To be able to pull something already made out of the fridge, warm it up, and set it on the table without much thought is a blessing! Enjoying the excess of provision fills the need and affirms the Father heart of God. It is His desire to take care of us, and yet at times, we can take the position of outcast, only relying on what is left over to meet us instead of looking to God as our source.

Boaz appealed to Ruth saying, *"Don't go to any other fields"* (Ruth 2:8). In other words, don't go looking for something better because the favor is here. Boaz is aware of Ruth's past; he has seen her faithfulness to Naomi and her work ethic.

In tough economic times, whether personally or as a nation, God's Word to us is that He desires to provide. He knows the intricacy of our jobs, when we have been passed over for a promotion or simply when the ends don't meet. It's easy to trust in our jobs, an inheritance, or other family members, but ultimately, He is our source. He will supply all that we need according to His riches, *not* according to our budget. All those other resources are pieces of the provision that is in His name.

> *²⁸ And why worry about your clothing? Look at the lilies of the field and how they grow. They don't work or make their clothing, ²⁹ yet Solomon in all his glory was not dressed as beautifully as they are. ³⁰ And if God cares so wonderfully for wildflowers that are here today and thrown into the fire tomorrow, he will certainly care for you. Why do you have so little faith?* (Matt. 6:28–29, NLT)

> *Some trust in chariots, some in horses but we will remember (trust) name of the Lord our God.* (Ps. 20:7, NKJV)

And His name is Jehovah Jirah, our provider!

No Longer Slaves

Boaz refers to Ruth as a daughter. In the natural, it is more than likely a reference to their age difference than a literal reference. I also believe it is a reference to the need of being a daughter or family member to share in the benefits of redemption. Our identity plays a huge role in how we receive the goodness of God. In reality, Ruth is a foreigner and subject to minimal care. She does not have to be included with the harvesters of Boaz, and yet he makes provision for her to be taken care of completely. Isn't that what Jesus did for us? He reached over the lines of the law and afforded us every gift.

> *"Think of it this way. If a father dies and leaves an inheritance for his young children, those children are not much better off than slaves until they grow up, even though they actually own everything their father had. ² They have to obey their guardians until they reach whatever age their*

father set. ³ And that's the way it was with us before Christ came. We were like children; we were slaves to the basic spiritual principles of this world.

⁴ But when the right time came, God sent his Son, born of a woman, subject to the law. ⁵ God sent him to buy freedom for us who were slaves to the law, so that he could adopt us as his very own children. ⁶ And because we are his children, God has sent the Spirit of his Son into our hearts, prompting us to call out, "Abba, Father." ⁷ Now you are no longer a slave but God's own child. And since you are his child, God has made you his heir." (Gal. 4:1–7, NLT)

We may "know" this intellectually, but let it sink in that we are His and He only desires the best for us. As His children, He watches out for us. He speaks to us kindly and to the heart of the matter. He does not focus on where we come from but directs us to where we are going. He pays attention to our service in His name and rewards us. He is our Father who sees our work as it glorifies Him.

Father God,

I confess that the process I am walking through in the fields of preparation is hard for me, so I lean on You and Your grace. I ask You to purify my heart, cleanse me from the wrong attitudes that would exalt my desires above your purposes. As a daughter, I look to You to supply my every need because You care and see all my needs. I give You all my service, for it is my desire to bring You glory. I give You praise, Jesus, for all that You are redeeming.

In Your name, Amen.

Professions of Faith: Chapter 5

1. Have you ever had someone be kind to you, treating you like family, but you felt unworthy? What does that uncover about your willingness to receive God's best?

_____

_____

2. According to Matthew 6:25–34, what should we seek after?

_____

_____

3. Read 2 Corinthians 1:19–22. After reading this passage, what are the conditions of His promises? How are they worked out?

_____

_____

4. Read Psalm 65:8–10, 1 Corinthians 2:9–10, and Ephesians 2:10. What do these passages say about preparation?

_____

_____

Chapter 6
No Weeping, No Reaping

¹⁴ Now Boaz said to her at mealtime, "Come here, and eat of the bread, and dip your piece of bread in the vinegar." So she sat beside the reapers, and he passed parched grain to her; and she ate and was satisfied, and kept some back. ¹⁵ And when she rose up to glean, Boaz commanded his young men, saying, "Let her glean even among the sheaves, and do not reproach her. ¹⁶ Also let grain from the bundles fall purposely for her; leave it that she may glean, and do not rebuke her."

¹⁷ So she gleaned in the field until evening, and beat out what she had gleaned, and it was about an ephah of barley. ¹⁸ Then she took it up and went into the city, and her mother-in-law saw what she had gleaned.

So she brought out and gave to her what she had kept back after she had been satisfied.

¹⁹ And her mother-in-law said to her, "Where have you gleaned today? And where did you work? Blessed be the one who took notice of you."

So she told her mother-in-law with whom she had worked, and said, "The man's name with whom I worked today is Boaz."

[20] Then Naomi said to her daughter-in-law, "Blessed be he of the LORD, who has not forsaken His kindness to the living and the dead!" And Naomi said to her, "This man is a relation of ours, one of our close relatives."

[21] Ruth the Moabitess said, "He also said to me, 'You shall stay close by my young men until they have finished all my harvest.'"

[22] And Naomi said to Ruth her daughter-in-law, "It is good, my daughter, that you go out with his young women, and that people do not meet you in any other field." [23] So she stayed close by the young women of Boaz, to glean until the end of barley harvest and wheat harvest; and she dwelt with her mother-in-law. (Ruth 2:14–23, NKJV)

In the early years of our marriage and ministry, Paul and I met with many days of meager provision. I am not complaining because the Lord always met our needs. We were never hungry and slept very comfortably. However, there were times at the grocery store that I was forced to be somewhat selective with my choices of fare. Going to the movie theater was a rarity, and fast food or a fancy restaurant happened only if we shared plates of food. But we learned to be grateful, and our extended family was more than generous, as we enjoyed wonderful vacations with little sacrifice. It was a long season that taught us to look to the Lord for provision, learning to pray bold prayers when we were in need, crying out to Him based on His goodness and not what we deserved.

I am forever imprinted with such a time when in foolish decision-making, we were climbing out of debt, and I felt the Lord impress on my heart to ask Him to meet this need. It went against everything my responsible self believed in. I mused, is it even right to ask God to bail you out of stupid choices? Nevertheless, I took a chance and began to contend for the lack. Months went by, and instead of becoming discouraged through tears, my faith was rising. Each time I brought it to His throne, my confidence grew as I appealed to His character. We were not worthy of a redeemed credit score, but the finished work of the Cross overshadowed the debt. To our amazement a miracle happened that met the balance due. God may deliver you differently, but I know He wants to. He may do it by different means, but God will roll His sleeves up when He is ready to save. Even now, years later, my eyes fill with tears at God's grace to allow me to harvest when I should have, at best, been only able to glean.

I can only wonder if Ruth felt that way as Boaz invited her to sit with him among the harvesters at lunch. She was unworthy—a foreigner and an outcast of society. He went a step further and instructed his workers to allow extra grain to fall for Ruth to pick up as she gleaned. In the evening when Ruth returned home to Naomi, she presented the grain and also leftovers from lunch—a supernatural doggy bag from the "Boaz Bistro." Pleased to hear about Ruth's day, Naomi inquired about whose field she has worked in and was delighted to find out it was Boaz. He was a family member with the ability to redeem their lost estate, according to Jewish heritage. Naomi, seeing God's hand, affirmed Ruth to continue to glean with the workers of Boaz, not only through barley harvest, but on through the wheat harvest.

Redeeming Relatives

According to the laws of the Pentateuch, a kinsman redeemer was a male relative who had the privilege or responsibility to provide for or protect on their behalf. In Hebrew the word is *ga'al (Strong's 1350): to redeem, buy back a relative's property (marry his widow), avenge, deliver, purchase, ransom.*

There were four qualifications necessary for a man to fulfill the role of kinsman redeemer (Lev. 25:47–49).

1. He must be a kinsman or related to the one he is going to buy back from slavery and/or purchase the estate.
2. He must be free himself from any debt or bondage.
3. He must be able to pay the price.
4. He must be willing to pay the price. A kinsman may have the finances but may not be willing to sacrifice them or want to turn the land over to an heir once the time came.

Boaz graciously asked Ruth to sit with him and his workers for lunch. This is a kindness not every gleaner would enjoy, especially one who was considered a foreigner. As the world becomes smaller and the mingling of people groups closer, it would seem that we could draw lines of boundary, based on kindness. Sadly, even with an abundance of teaching on tolerance and acceptance, we still find ourselves at odds with cultures we don't understand. I am not going to attempt to answer all of the questions of society or even a few for that matter because they are complex. I do know the enemy loves division, feeds on fear, and promotes lies. Satan enjoys when our unique qualities become distorted into factions and deception leads to fear. Instead of embracing the purposes of God's creativity in design, there is a perversion of truth. Ultimately, it will disintegrate into a lack of trust, resulting in heart motivations being judged. Thankfully there are those, like Boaz, who will look beyond a culture to see what God desires.

Silent Night

In the Battle of the Bulge in World War II, a German soldier hid his family in a shack away from the battlefield. It was not uncommon for soldiers to become lost in dark woods during fierce fighting and become separated from their units. It was Christmas Eve, and the young German soldier's family prepared to partake of the chicken dinner cooked by his wife. There was a knock at the door as three American soldiers asked if they could come in. As they waited to partake in the supper, another knock rang out, only this time, it was four German soldiers. The lady explained that the Americans were guests, and if they were to enter they would need to lay down their weapons. They agreed and after some awkward silence, an American fighter offered some cigarettes that eventually led to singing "Silent Night." After the meal, the German soldiers even treated one of the injured Americans. They slept under the same roof that night, and in the morning, the Germans explained to the Americans the way back to their unit. Kindness! What a beautiful picture of the grace of our Savior, on the night they celebrated His birth, love was shown. The very reason He came was manifest in a night of peace, instead of hostility.

> *You prepare a feast for me*
> *in the presence of my enemies.*
> *You honor me by anointing my head with oil.*
> *My cup overflows with blessing.* (Ps. 23:5, NLT)

Humans have the ability to show intense hatred to one another, but I believe with the Lord of love living within our hearts, we have a greater ability to show charity, grace, and concern. It is this redemptive purpose that changes history, releasing a blessing that becomes a heritage of kindness.

Satisfaction Guaranteed

I'm sure at least one time you have gone to a restaurant, expecting an amazing meal, only to walk away disappointed by the food, service, and maybe even the atmosphere. I had an experience one time where I had planned to meet my Sistas (a group of close friends of more than twenty-five-plus years). I arrived a little earlier than the others and put my name in and how many of us there would be. The hostess graciously seated me and confirmed they would be watching for the rest of my group. I sat in the back of the restaurant about thirty minutes when I decided to give one of the ladies a call. She then proceeded to ask where I was. I told her I had been at the restaurant, seated and waiting for them. Somehow, they had already been seated at a different area of the establishment with no idea that I was there waiting. Frustrated, I found them, and I must have shown that I was also flustered because after a few minutes, the manager came and kindly gave me a gift card for my trouble. Even in what I believed to be poor attention to service, I was satisfied by their desire to remedy my disappointment.

Boaz exceeded Ruth's expectations by carefully attending to her needs and overwhelmed her with abundance. He modeled the true heart of Father God who sets us up for blessing because He longs to satisfy us. Abba looks at the state of His lowly servants and fills them with good things (Luke 1), orchestrating creation to find them. But we must ask ourselves, "What do I believe, are my expectations in past circumstances or do I hope in the Lord, and how have my past disappointments framed my thoughts about God?" Even in the midst of possible conflict or potential disappointment, Ruth was contented at the table of Boaz, receiving a blessing she did not anticipate.

The Bible is chock full of examples related to satisfaction. In fact, one of the names of God is El Shaddai or "all sufficient one." It is in His character to fill us, to give us more than enough. *He is our portion*; by His hand He brings prosperity (Gen. 41:29), in His presence we have fullness of joy (Ps. 16:11), and He desires to give us a full life (Job 42:17).

> *He will comfort us and make us rejoice. He will fill to the full our souls with abundance, satisfying us with His goodness. Refrain from weeping and tears for your work in due season will be rewarded. Your children will come*

back from the lands of the enemy for there is hope in your future. (Jer. 31:13–17, paraphrased)

Recently, I found myself traveling in an area where Paul and I had spent many years with our family. As I drove, I began experiencing a feeling of regret and grief. Through the sadness, I began to ponder the "what ifs" and how my life might have been on a different course if only the choices made were different. I have cried and cried and cried about these same issues of life, the unending and disappointing circumstances over and over again, holding on as they sifted through my hands like sand. While I meandered through town, I breathed my prayers and, shedding a few tears, let go of my losses. I tend to be a slow learner, for the Lord has spoken gently to me a few times before saying, "It is done; release it into my hands."

"You have taken account of my wanderings;
Put my tears in Your bottle.
Are they not recorded in Your book?

Then my enemies will turn back in the day when I call;
This I know, that God is for me.

In God, whose word I praise,
In the Lord, *whose word I praise.* (Ps. 56:8–10, AMP)

We may be slow learners, even stubborn at times, but God takes notice of our sorrow. We might tell others or even ourselves to "get over it!" Yet the Lord responds with patience and kindness. He maps every road we travel like an accountant meticulously records transactions in a ledger. We may feel lost, but He knows right where we are! We are so precious to Father God that He preserves our tears in bottles; each one kept as a remembrance in the courts of heaven. When the enemy tries to steal our life with discouragement, disqualify us with lies, and obscure the path before us with confusion, the Psalmist reminds us that "God is for us," and if "God is for us, who can be against us? (Rom. 8:31–39).

Research has indicated a fascinating fact; a single tear has unique components making each drop one of a kind, like a seed that, when planted in the fertile soil of a tender heart, will yield a crop of confidence in our relationship with Jesus and a fruitful work of the Spirit. *"Those who sow in tears shall reap in joy ... bearing seed for sowing"* (Ps. 126:5–6, NKJV). Sow your tears; make them count for kingdom purpose, with the promise in knowing that you will reap in joy!

No doubt Ruth shed a few tears in her fields, but she moved on in purpose, and God rewarded her work.

Interestingly, one of the definitions for the word *satisfy* is *weary*.

I confess that there are many times I am weary or tired of my troubles.

"*¹⁷ So she gleaned in the field until evening, and beat out what she had gleaned, and it was about an ephah of barley*" (Ruth 2:17, NKJV). However, the choice is still up to us what type of crop we will harvest.

You Reap What You Sow

People close to me know that I do not have a green thumb. Plants have a short lifespan around me; it is not in my skill set, and I admire those that can tend to a garden, eventually partaking of its yield. Lately, I have been contemplating what it means to harvest what I have sown. I have chosen to listen to an audio Bible in addition to reading this past year, and hearing the spoken Word has given me a different perspective. My ears opened as revelation has come in a new way. One day, as the narrator read Hebrews 12, I heard it—I really heard it, and all of the sudden I felt as if it was reading me and exposing little flaws in my planting: *"See to it that no one comes short of the grace of God;*

*that no **root of bitterness** springing up causes trouble, and by it many be defiled"* (Heb. 12:15, NASB).

I began to think of some recent disappointments, regrets, and even what I deemed unfair treatment. It's amazing that what happened years ago can suddenly spring up and expose skeletons as if it were an archeological dig. Frankly, I was a little confused! How many times had I been prayed over with deliverance prayers, cried and confessed my faults, and to settle things, I declared blessing over my bad experiences? But I know the nudging of the Spirit to dig deeper, like an archeologist gently stroking a brush to expose something hidden in the earth. He does not seek to damage us, but to show the framework of the artifact, revealing the unseen treasure. I thought of the legacy I want to leave, not only for my children, but in them. What will they sow? The scripture impacted me with the phrase; "and by it many become defiled." As the spoken Word filled the air, it gripped my heart and conviction gripped my soul.

I realized destruction is the fruit when bitterness is nurtured and eventually the fruit of it reaped in the hearts of my children, and that would be my legacy. Every time I respond to frustration with complaints or disillusionment with cynicism, I cast unhealthy seed into the soil of the heart. The choice is mine, and sadly, I have chosen poorly in the past, allowing my discontent to rule and feed my weariness. This not only draws attention to what is lacking, but it erodes faith with questions that cause one to doubt the goodness of God in life. This is an ancient trick of the enemy to make us think that the Lord is withholding provision, and once we have full disclosure of the situation, we would see that God is unable to satiate our desires. That is a lie Satan is very good at telling since he has used it from the dawn of creation, simply tweaking it according to our unique perspective.

We can be full of disappointment in our circumstances to the point we are left dissatisfied with God, our focus turned away from Him, shining a spotlight, exposing the weeds that choke out the fruit of the Spirit. If we become weary, chances are, we would become complacent and give up, no longer moving in the direction of all that God planned for us in the field ripe for harvest. I am not just talking about a monetary gain; I am speaking to the times when a loved one is just ready to surrender to salvation, and we undermine it by saying the wrong thing or the times we give up on our spouse just before the reconciliation. I'm certain you have thoughts of your weary return and you cry out like the prophet Habakkuk with "How long, Lord?"

*"I entreated Your favor with my whole heart; be merciful to me according to Your word. I thought about my ways, **and turned my feet to Your testimonies**"* (Ps. 119:58–59, NKJV).

By all means, cry, plead, and call upon the Lord! Request His favor and then do your part; turn your feet or actions to the past days when you have witnessed God intervening on your behalf. In my own prayer times, I have actually done a prophetic act by sharing my heart with the Lord and then turning around and declaring His past deliverance as it played out in my life. Our attitude will determine the type of crop we will yield and whether we will harvest or continue to glean.

Harvest Time

> *[15] And when she rose up to glean, Boaz commanded his young men, saying, "Let her glean even among the sheaves, and do not reproach her. [16] Also let grain from the bundles fall purposely for her; leave it that she may glean, and do not rebuke her."*
>
> *[17] So she gleaned in the field until evening, and beat out what she had gleaned, and it was about an ephah of barley.* (Ruth 2:15–17, NKJV)

In her gleaning, Ruth was truly harvesting. It is significant to the point that Naomi took notice of the abundance. Hope was rising, and faith was being renewed; maybe Naomi was beginning to remember her true name and identity.

I can almost picture it: Ruth was sharing about her day while unloading the groceries, and Naomi asked, "Just where did you glean today?" Ruth responded, "I was encouraged to glean in the field of Boaz; in fact, he told me to continue to work there from now on." Naomi knew who Boaz was and was stirred by what she perceives to be the pieces of recovery coming together, so she offers praise to God for He has remembered His covenant to His people and has opened a door that may lead to redemption!

> *[21] Ruth the Moabitess said, "He also said to me, 'You shall stay close by my young men until they have finished all my harvest.'"*
>
> *[22] And Naomi said to Ruth her daughter-in-law, "It is good, my daughter, that you go out with his young women, and that people do not meet you in any other field." [23] So she stayed close by the young women of Boaz, to glean until the end of barley harvest and wheat harvest; and she dwelt with her mother-in-law.* (Ruth 2:14–23, NKJV)

Things are changing, so much so that Ruth is encouraged by Naomi to follow and stay close to the young women of Boaz. It is good that she stay in his field to glean for more reasons than what they can see in the natural.

"And now, dear brothers and sisters, one final thing. Fix your thoughts on what is true, and honorable, and right, and pure, and lovely, and admirable. Think about things that are excellent and worthy of praise" (Phil. 4:8, NLT). Our thoughts have a great deal to do with our character and conduct. The company we keep has input into our thoughts by way of our conversations with them. Then we meditate on those

thoughts, potentially affecting our moods and eventually leading to actions. We can venture into fields of unbelief and lack, fields of gossip, envy, strife, unwholesome talk, and jealousy. All of these start as small foxes that spoil the vine, ultimately resulting in little or no fruit.

Sadly, it is all too easy to enter into conversation that does little to edify and becomes a slippery slope when encouraged by friends. We are told to "fix our thoughts" on virtuous things, in other words, cement them in the Word! It is an act of faith to recognize a struggle and choose to believe the best but takes no restraint to see a problem and complain. Toxic relationships can sneak up on us; one minute we are committed to doing great things together, and in the next moment, all the life within us is drained. All it takes is our focus to switch from gratitude to pessimism. God calls His children to a higher level of resolve. Through His Word, the power of His Spirit, and our choice to partner with Him, our thoughts will line up with His.

Naomi praises God for leading Ruth to Boaz, a close relative, or kinsman-redeemer (Ps. 111:9). Things are turning around for the better. Boaz is a type of Christ or an example of the work Jesus will fulfill later in time. If you know Jesus as your Messiah, Lord, and Savior, you have already received this benefit! The Old Testament is gloriously tethered to the New as we see the love of God fulfilled in the complete work of Jesus!

> *[16] We also know that the Son did not come to help angels; he came to help the descendants of Abraham. [17] Therefore, it was necessary for him to be made in every respect like us, his brothers and sisters, so that he could be our merciful and faithful High Priest before God. Then he could offer a sacrifice that would take away the sins of the people. [18] Since he himself has gone through suffering and testing, he is able to help us when we are being tested.* (Heb. 2:16–18, NLT)

In every way, Jesus fulfilled the requirements of our kinsman-redeemer:

1. He became a kinsman. God is both eternal life and the source of life, so it is impossible for Him to save us without the incarnation of Christ. Jesus was born a man—"made like His brothers"—and took on flesh in order to experience death for us (Heb. 2:17).

2. He was free from the bondage of sin. We have been in bondage to sin from the day Adam and Eve sinned in the garden. Only Jesus could set us free (Heb. 2:14–15).

3. He was able to pay the ransom price. Even if there had been another perfect man, he would have only been able to redeem one man. Jesus being fully man and fully God was able to redeem all of mankind (John 1:29–31).

4. He was willing to pay the price. This is the most exciting, amazing, and humbling truth of all. Even while we were still in our sin, Jesus died for us (Rom. 5:6–9). No one took it from Him, He willingly gave it. And there was only one reason: *love*. This is what led the theologian Karl Barth to proclaim: "Jesus loves me this I know, for the Bible tells me so."

Take a moment right now and thank Him. Give Jesus the praise He deserves! If you don't know Jesus as your personal Savior and Redeemer or you have simply want to rededicate your heart in a fresh way, ask Him to come into your life right now. He is standing at the door, waiting for the invitation to be a part of your daily walk.

Ruth had met her redeemer. He was both kind and generous, and his name was Boaz. It was only the beginning of an incredible journey being led by a God who keeps His Word.

Father,

I confess that there are times I am weary of the fields I walk. I choose to sow my tears, knowing in due season

I will reap in joy. I refuse to listen to any counsel that would undermine Your truth, so please help me to be careful of the company I surround myself with. I thank you that all is not lost because my Redeemer lives, and His name is Jesus. I thank you, Jesus, for being willing to be my sacrifice and buying back all of my worth. I love you with all my heart.

In Jesus's wonderful name, Amen!

Professions of Faith: Chapter 6

1. We have learned that we can sow our tears and reap a harvest. Read the following verses and write down other ways we can sow our tears: Genesis 33:4; 2 Kings 20:5, Esther 4:1–3, Isaiah 42:14, Joel 2:12–13, and John 11:35.

_____

_____

_____

_____

_____

_____

_____

2. As we are studying the book of Ruth, what are some parallels we see in her life and Psalm 23?

_____

_____

_____

3. Read Proverbs 16:3 and Luke 1:46–55, especially verse 51. How do our thoughts and imaginations affect our redemptive harvest? What should our response be?

_____

_____

Chapter 7
Casting Away the Past for Anointed Substance

Then Naomi her mother-in-law said to her, "My daughter, shall I not seek security for you, that it may be well with you? ² Now Boaz, whose young women you were with, is he not our relative? In fact, he is winnowing barley tonight at the threshing floor. ³ Therefore wash yourself and anoint yourself, put on your best garment and go down to the threshing floor; but do not make yourself known to the man until he has finished eating and drinking. ⁴ Then it shall be, when he lies down, that you shall notice the place where he lies; and you shall go in, uncover his feet, and lie down; and he will tell you what you should do."

⁵ And she said to her, "All that you say to me I will do." (Ruth 3:1–5, NKJV)

The light had begun to return to her countenance as hope was rising in Naomi due to a shift in circumstances. You can begin to hear intention in Naomi's voice as chance had made way to purpose. She recognized that there was more at play than fate and devised a plan. Boaz was a declared relative with the ability to redeem the lost estate, and he was winnowing on the threshing floor. Naomi directed Ruth to wash and anoint herself, making herself ready to return to Boaz as he threshed the grain.

The Threshing Floor

The threshing floor was a flat piece of land, an ideal location used for separating grain from the chaff (Isa. 1:15; Deut. 25:4; Judg. 6:11). Wind was needed for this process, so the place was usually at the top of a hill or an open field. Sometimes the floor was cut out of a rock. Threshing floors were watched all night to guard against thieves and were considered very valuable. At times, they were considered a place for memoriam or meeting places (Gen. 50:10; 1 Kgs. 22:10; 2 Sam. 6:6).

Symbolically, the threshing floor represents the place a relationship between the bride and the bridegroom is established. Naomi instructed Ruth to go to Boaz at the threshing floor. Boaz is a type or symbolic of Christ, the Bridegroom, and Ruth is symbolic of the church, His Bride. So it is with great purpose that Ruth met him there.

The process on the threshing floor begins with stalks of grain that were dried and placed on the rock(s) to be either trampled over by oxen or beaten with the threshing sledge.

The second step on the threshing floor involves winnowing, a process in which grain is extracted after the husk is removed. The husk is cracked open by the trampling of the animals. When the wind picks up, the grain is cast into the air where the breeze carries the lightweight husk (chaff) and blows it away. The grain falls to the ground where it is gathered, scooped up, and put into baskets, then stored.

It is at the threshing floor where the fruit or productivity of our lives is laid down in an act of obedience and humility. Father God takes this opportunity to strip away anything that is useless for His kingdom. He will use circumstances, jobs, and people, especially the Body of Christ, our brothers and sisters. Have you ever been serving the Lord and felt as if someone close is grating on you, even trampling over your gifts? Be encouraged; your works are being purified! The worthless exterior is being broken down in order for mature fruit (or grain) to be exposed. The process is not yet finished, the husk or lightweight material must be tossed, and the flesh must give way to the Spirit. Our gifts and talents must be cast into the air, along with our superficiality. We may feel discarded, when in reality, God is getting to the good stuff. He gently blows the wind of the Spirit to allow what is pure to remain. *"As iron sharpens iron, a friend sharpens a friend"* (Prov. 27:17, NLT).

Bad Fruit

Many years ago the church we were attending was in need of janitor services, and due to some financial challenges, they would be unable to compensate this position monetarily. I felt impressed on my heart that my husband and I would help serve in this capacity by cleaning the restrooms. We would come in weekly to clean the evening before Sunday services with very few knowing we were the ones serving. However, one week we came ready to provide our services when we walked in on a deacon finishing up what was ours to do. Embarrassingly, I admit I was not happy that our opportunity to clean had been taken from us. My husband, on the other hand, joyfully accepted this provision. A few days later, after the dust settled (and the cleanser dissipated), I recognized the nudging of the Spirit to address my attitude.

What was the big deal? I was just acting righteously to an injustice. It was my word that was infringed upon and an opportunity to serve was taken away, or so I told myself. I inquired of the Lord, "Why is my position on this subject wrong?" I argued my case further: "They should let us know if someone else is going to take over. We took time out of our evening only to find it was already done!" Finally, when my rant was finished, the Lord gently spoke to my spirit, "What does it matter who cleans? The church body was taken care of and isn't that the point?" He pressed further in my thoughts, "Maybe your motivation was about you more than meeting the needs of the congregation." Even though my intention initially was to be a blessing it was my actions that spoke louder. My words expressed control and a desire to be significant; neither are the actions of a servant leader. The Lord was threshing out and exposing the quality of my fruit.

We are not only a participant in this process, but we also partner with God to perform His will in each other and on the earth.

> *"14 Do not be afraid, you worm Jacob,*
> *little Israel, do not fear,*
> *for I myself will help you," declares the Lord,*
> *your Redeemer, the Holy One of Israel.*
> *15 "See, I will make you into a threshing sledge,*
> *new and sharp, with many teeth.*
> *You will thresh the mountains and crush them,*
> *and reduce the hills to chaff.*
> *16 You will winnow them, the wind will pick them up,*
> *and a gale will blow them away.*
> *But you will rejoice in the Lord*
> *and glory in the Holy One of Israel."* (Isa. 41:14–16, NIV)

Our time on the threshing floor is not wasted, nor is it only for perfecting our motives. Look closely at verse 15: *"You will thresh the mountains and crush them."* Some other translations say "make them small." The mountains, many times in scripture, represent obstacles (Isa. 40:4). They come in all shapes and sizes, both literally and figuratively.

On the threshing floor, God is fashioning each one of us into a well-equipped instrument that will bring down the obstacles that hinder His kingdom. Does this mean we go around tearing down others with our words, ministries with our critical approach, or issues in our families with loveless boundaries? Of course not! One of the most powerful weapons in our arsenal is intercession. When we bring Spirit-led information to the throne of God, our prayers partner with His purpose and chip away at what is obstructing vision. As we ask for direction, He is faithful to speak to us concerning our problems! The Word of God, declared in authority and faith over a barrier, will bring order in a fashion similar to the Lord speaking His Word over creation. Problems arise because we tend to declare what we want in our limited understanding instead of discerning what the Lord wants. His ways and thoughts are higher; therefore, instead of resigning to our earthly situations and ideas, we should ask Him for the mind of Christ that will elevate our thinking into the heavenly realms.

Many things will try to lift themselves up above what we know of God. We do not wage war with worldly weapons, but with God's mighty weapons, we break down every proud, rebellious argument (2 Cor. 10:3–6) that keeps people from knowing God. The more we experience the presence of God through hills and valleys, the better equipped we are to destroy strongholds. It's not by might or power, but by His Spirit (Zech. 4:6), and it's also through trust, believing that God is bigger than our mountains. Most of the time, the battlefield is our own thought process built upon a foundation of deception, reinforced through emotional ties, and cemented in familiarity. The more the Spirit tries to shape my identity with truth, the tighter the grip of reality is exposed in my actions, and I feel like I am spinning on an out-of-control potter's wheel. I may feel my life is in chaos, but if I am yielded to the Spirit's work, resolution is a prayer away. I expressed one such experience in this journal entry:

> I felt the Lord speaking to me today saying, "You are crying in the wilderness, and your intercession is preparing the way. In all your ways acknowledge me (walk upright and good), and I will make your paths clear. The way you walk in the desert is creating a path for God. Your valley will be exalted and the mountains and hills, all the high places in your life are being humbled (Isa. 15). The crooked places, the iniquities, are being straightened out at this time. The rough edges of your personality are softening. My glory shall be uncovered like treasures in darkness, this treasure in your dark time as riches hidden in secret places. I am the Lord who has called you by name. Stop striving with me and trust what I am making you to be."

A journal entry from 11/2/01 (based on Isa. 40:3–5; Prov. 3:6; Isa. 45:1–9).

In our natural sight we cannot see the finished result, but God does. He sees the end from the beginning. Not only does He have our past in view, but He is already in our future, calling us forward and cheering us on to our higher calling in Christ Jesus. *In perspective, it is our intercession that breaks down barriers by agreeing with God's plans and declaring purpose, but it is grace that turns that mountain of regret into a heap of possibility.* In those times of wishing we could have done something better, relying on our good works to bring down what looms before us, we become burdened by our works. The peak is just too high to climb on our own, so call upon His grace because HE is *sufficient*—ample in amount, fit in character, and competent (Strongs Greek 2425) to arrive at the right time. Better yet, activate your intercession with grace and speak to the mountain.

*"This is the word of the L*ORD *to Zerubbabel:*
'Not by might nor by power, but by My Spirit,'
*Says the L*ORD *of hosts.*
⁷ 'Who are you, O great mountain?
Before Zerubbabel you shall become a plain!
And he shall bring forth the capstone
With shouts of "Grace, grace to it!" (Zech. 4:6–7, NKJV)

Something Familiar

It seems the deeper the valley and the taller the mountain, the more difficult it is to walk anywhere else. We know that road well; it is familiar and although not the healthiest road, it strangely brings comfort. Our disappointments become like a funeral dirge we have rehearsed a thousand times and gives us reasons to justify our complacency. So instead of conquering, we circle the mountain and do whatever it takes to avoid hiking through the valley.

I confess I have stayed that course longer than needed.

The children of Israel walked in similar circumstances, staying on a path for forty years when the distance to the Promised Land should have taken days. Unfortunately, they were stubborn and sinful, complaining about their situation (Deut. 9:7, 24, 27). They failed to trust God to bring them to the place of promise. So God led them on a path of humility until He deemed the process complete. *"² And the Lord spoke to me, saying, ³ 'You have **circled** this mountain long enough. Now turn north"* (Deut. 2:2–3, NASB).

Perhaps the biggest obstacle in the way was their mind-set, which led to incessant complaining. They forgot the miracles that He performed to keep them safe on the journey, providing for their needs and guiding them through obstacles along the way, and they allowed fear to cloud their eyes while in full view of blessings. They became desirous of captivity and in their hearts were envious of the past. *"Why has the Lord brought us to this land to fall by the sword, that our wives and children should become **victims**? Would it not be better for us to return to Egypt?"* (Deut.14:3, NKJV).

I know, as a parent, how it feels when I have given an opportunity for an extraordinary gift and the receiver is not too appreciative—but really?! First, they cried about being slaves, and now they are crying about the conditions concerning their freedom. Fear had replaced faith, so the Promise Land would not be realized their lifetime. *"But your little ones, whom you said would be **victims**, I will bring in, and they shall know the land which you have despised"* (Deut. 14:31, NKJV).

A whole generation missed seeing the fulfillment of God's faithfulness in the wilderness due to their complaining and disobedience. How much have I lost due to a victim mentality? How much peace do I forfeit, worrying about something that may or may not happen? Walking into new territory can be unnerving, but God had told them that they would not be alone, and He confirmed it through His actions over and over by repeatedly delivering, feeding, and clothing them. Their disobedience and sin had caused them to forfeit the promise, but living in fear would leave them with regret. He was faithful to His Word and desired a people that would have an undivided heart toward Him. He is a good God and deserving of their trust and praise.

*Bless the L*ORD*, O my soul,*
And all that is within me, bless His holy name.
*² Bless the L*ORD*, O my soul,*
And forget none of His benefits. (Ps. 103:1–2, NASB)
*I will bless the Lord **at all times**; His praise shall continually be in my mouth.* (Ps. 34:1, NASB)

The more we give voice to our fear, the more we wander in our doubt, and resentment is not far off the beaten path. God will more than make up for what we believe is missing from our lives, but we must take Him at His Word. We must discipline ourselves and choose to trust in His plan by replacing complaints with praise and disappointment with gratitude. That is not an easy decision, but it is one that will result in blessing, and we will see that the longings in our heart are honored with the fulfillment of God's purpose.

One Step at a Time

> *"Therefore wash yourself and anoint yourself, put on your best garment and go down to the threshing floor; but do not make yourself known to the man until he has finished eating and drinking"* (Ruth 3:3).

The time of mourning is complete for Ruth; it is time for her to rise up, wash, and anoint herself for a new day. A similar response is modeled in 2 Samuel 12:15b–23; we read of the story of David after his sin with Bathsheba. Their first child together, a son, became ill, so David fasted and prayed crying out to God to spare him. However, the Lord in His wisdom took him home. In the finality of God's decision, scripture says that David arose and washed, changed his clothes, and anointed himself. Then he worshipped the Lord (vs. 20).

Obviously, my counsel here is not to rush us through a natural grieving process, but there is a way to move forward without denying the loss. Honestly, there are losses in different forms that will forever mark us and even redefine who we are, but they don't have to confine us. When God declares a process as complete for that season, it is in our best interest to trust His redeeming work and take a step forward.

Jesus conquered death, hell, and the grave in order to redeem or buy back all that was lost. In Luke 24:5, the women at the tomb of Jesus were asked, "Why do you seek the living among the dead"? It is an interesting question, considering that they were at a tomb. Even though we have the privilege of being in the future of such events and know our Jesus was already resurrected at that point, I believe it holds a beautiful promise. When our dreams, hopes, and expectations have died, I perceive the Lord saying, "Seek the life within the death." The desires of our heart-represented in dreams, expectations and hopes may be buried in the darkest crypt, but it is only a temporary resting place. In Psalm 16:9–11, David declares, "You will not allow your Holy one to see corruption," Jesus didn't stay there to the point of decay, and neither will your destiny. The results of your vision may not look entirely the same. As grief brings about a natural re-invention of those left in this life, God re-forms our crumbled heap of desires by shaping them with value and compassion. During the process, we may find comfort in trying to figure out the reasons for delayed plans, broken relationships, lost jobs, and shattered dreams, but ultimately our peace lies in the person of Jesus who paid the price in order for it to be redeemed.

> *³ Blessed be the God and Father of our Lord Jesus Christ, who according to His abundant mercy has begotten us again to a **living hope** through the resurrection of Jesus Christ from the dead, ⁴ to an **inheritance incorruptible and undefiled** and that does not fade away, reserved in*

> *heaven for you, ⁵ who are kept by the power of God through faith for salvation ready to be revealed in the last time.*
>
> *⁶ In this you greatly rejoice, though now for a little while, if need be, you have been* **grieved by various trials**, *⁷ that the genuineness of your faith, being much more precious than gold that perishes, though it is tested by fire, may be found to praise, honor, and glory at the revelation of Jesus Christ, ⁸ whom having not seen you love.* **Though now you do not see Him, yet believing***, you rejoice with joy inexpressible and full of glory, ⁹ receiving the end of your faith—the salvation of your souls.* (1 Pet. 1:3–9, NKJV)

Although it may take some time, we also receive hope when we adopt an eternal perspective. We don't grieve the same as those who don't know the Lord. In 2 Samuel 12:23, David expresses his hope to be with his son again in heaven. He understands that life here is temporary, but with the Lord life is eternal.

David also shows us by example a process that may help us move on when life already has.

He washed: The work of Holy Spirit allows a renovation in our mind that adjusts our way of thinking and gives us vision for life. God may not have sanctioned the loss, but He hasn't left us to stay there; His Spirit adjusts our perspective and purpose to fulfill the plans for our lives (Titus 3:4–5).

He changed his clothes: We wear different types of clothes for different occasions: working in the yard, church, funerals, parties, and so on. Our minds adjust with the correlating event. Sometimes, we need to change our "mourning" garments into "garments of praise" so that our thoughts are in line. It's not that we have arrived, but we are further than we used to be, and for that we can certainly be thankful (Isa. 61:3).

He anointed himself: We have been set apart by His anointing to go out to the oppressed and bring good news, comfort, and joy. The process in which anointing oil is prepared offers a glimpse into what is required in order to be anointed. Olives were pressed between heavy stones, more than once, in order for the oil to be extracted. All the "fleshy" material of the olive was removed to keep the oil pure. Spices were then added, including those used for burial. Quite a picture isn't it? Sometimes life is heavy with circumstances pressing in around us, and it is our choice whether we will die to self and be a pure fragrant offering (Luke 4:17–19).

He worshipped: Worship is more than singing a song; it can be a sacrifice. Putting God first expresses our trust in Him to do exceedingly abundantly more than we can imagine. Lifting up the Lord above our circumstances will cost us by causing us to set aside our wants, desires, comfort, and even emotions, but the fragrance released is pleasing to the Lord (John 12:3; 2 Sam. 24:23–25).

For some of us it may be a difficult choice to move forward. Thankfully, we have the Spirit of God anointing us for a new season and His Word to guide us along the way. He is faithfully leading us from death to life, from grief to joy, and from a spirit of heaviness to the substance of anointing.

Father,

I come to You in the name of my Redeemer, Jesus Christ. I exalt Your name above any argument in my mind to keep me bound to the way life used to be. I trust that as I release my past, you are making it into something of value and anointing me for a new season. I thank you that all that I have been through is a set up to bring joy and purpose to those around me.

In Jesus's name, Amen.

Professions of Faith: Chapter 7

1. Read Ephesians 3:8–19; list some benefits to overcoming obstacles in your life.

_____

_____

2. In Proverbs 27:17, we read how our relationships work to sharpen each other. Read Galatians 6:15. What are some of the requirements needed?

_____

_____

3. What are we called to, according to 1 Peter 3:8–12?

_____

_____

4. As unpleasant as the threshing floor can be, what are some of the benefits we discussed in this chapter? Any personal observations?

_____

_____

Chapter 8

Covered in Covenant

⁶ So she went down to the threshing floor and did according to all that her mother-in-law instructed her. ⁷ And after Boaz had eaten and drunk, and his heart was cheerful, he went to lie down at the end of the heap of grain; and she came softly, uncovered his feet, and lay down.

⁸ Now it happened at midnight that the man was startled, and turned himself; and there, a woman was lying at his feet. ⁹ And he said, "Who are you?"

So she answered, "I am Ruth, your maidservant. Take your maidservant under your wing, for you are a close relative."

¹⁰ Then he said, "Blessed are you of the LORD, my daughter! For you have shown more kindness at the end than at the beginning, in that you did not go after young men, whether poor or rich. ¹¹ And now, my daughter, do not fear. I will do for you all that you request, for all the people of my town know that you are a virtuous woman. ¹² Now it is true that I am a close relative; however, there is a relative closer than I. ¹³ Stay this night, and in the morning it shall be that if he will perform the duty of a close relative for you—good; let him do it. But if he does not want to perform the duty for you, then I will perform the duty for you, as the LORD lives! Lie down until morning."

⁴ So she lay at his feet until morning, and she arose before one could recognize another. Then he said, "Do not let it be known that the woman came to the threshing floor." ¹⁵ Also he said, "Bring the shawl that is on you and hold it." And when she held it, he measured six ephahs of barley, and laid it on her. Then she went into the city.

¹⁶ When she came to her mother-in-law, she said, "Is that you, my daughter?"

Then she told her all that the man had done for her. ¹⁷ And she said, "These six ephahs of barley he gave me; for he said to me, 'Do not go empty-handed to your mother-in-law.'"

¹⁸ Then she said, "Sit still, my daughter, until you know how the matter will turn out; for the man will not rest until he has concluded the matter this day.'" (Ruth 3:6–18, NKJV)

    Ruth obeyed Naomi and went down to the threshing floor. After Boaz had eaten and was satisfied, he lay down to rest at the end of a heap of grain. Quietly Ruth removed what would have likely have been his prayer shawl, uncovered his feet, and lay down next to him.
    Boaz awakened around midnight to discover a woman lying at his feet. Ruth identified herself and asked to be taken under his wing. Humbled by her proposal, Boaz explained that there was another in line with the ability to redeem, but he would look into the matter. Boaz was a righteous man and would take the appropriate steps to ensure her redemption. He was also concerned for her reputation and told her to stay. There was nothing inappropriate in the suggestion by Boaz; he was

simply trying to preserve Ruth's reputation. In the morning, he blessed her with a substantial amount of grain to take home to Naomi before the heat of the day. Ruth was encouraged to be still, for the matter would be settled.

Wing (Strong's H3671)-*Kanaph*: edge, extremity, border, corner, garment. At the edge of a garment or prayer shawl would have been fringes that would have been twisted together called *tzitzit*.

Under Your Wing: As explained in the culture of the Middle East, the term *under your wing* is symbolic of a marriage proposal by casting a garment over the one claimed for marriage. Ruth was asking for the ability to take refuge or cover in Boaz. This is extremely significant for Ruth because the corners of his garment would have been the fringes or *tzitzit*. The word *tzitzit* means to "blossom" or "bloom." As God's children, we are encouraged to bear fruit. It is on the branches where fruit or blossoms appear. *"I am the vine (source), you are the branches (extension). He who abides in me and I in him, bears much fruit; for without Me you can do nothing"* (John 15:5, NKJV).

Family Matters

Ruth is seeking marriage, but eventually she will be covered in covenant by Jehovah God. In today's culture, although it is acceptable to be married, it is unpopular for a woman to submit to a man to the extent that he is over her. Many times, a couple is married by ceremony alone with each living separate lives when God intended us to live "as one" (Mark 10:8). This does not mean either mate must relinquish personality, gifting, and desires, but it does mean we no longer live to satisfy only ourselves. We become a united front by living in a way that brings *completed* glory to God. She has seen His amazing love and wants to be a part of it. Ruth is being grafted in, just as we have been. *"Ten men from every language of the nations shall grasp the sleeve (lit. wing) of a Jewish man, saying 'Let us go with you, for we have heard that God is with you'"* (Zech. 8:23, NKJV).

In a Jewish wedding ceremony, the couple is married under a *huppah*, which is a decorative structure that is covered by the groom's prayer shawl. This symbolizes being under the protective cover of her husband, just as we are under the protective covering of God in Christ (Col. 3:3).

Keep me as the apple of your eye; hide me under the shadow of your wings. (Psalm 17:8, NKJV)

He shall cover you with His feathers, and under His wings you shall take refuge; His truth shall be your shield and buckler (small shield). (Ps. 91:4, NKJV)

But those who wait on the Lord shall renew their strength. (Isa. 40:31, NKJV)

Wait (Strong's H6960): to expect, look patiently, to tarry. Primitive root means to bind together or twist. This is suggesting the need to bind ourselves in relationship with God.

When the way is hidden, wait (bind) on Him. When you are tired, wait (twist) on Him. When all seems to be lost, wait (wrap) on Him.

Boaz was seeking a way to be a groom to his desired bride Ruth. We are God's desired bride, the church, and it is His plan and purpose for us to be joined and woven together in its structure. *"Let us not neglect meeting together ... but encourage one another"* (Heb. 10:25, NLT). God's design is for His people to come together in worship, teaching and bringing encouragement to one another.

There is also safety when we choose to come under authority. Giving ourselves to relationships in a local fellowship builds strong support systems that hold us up when we are walking through life's challenges and keeps us in check when we are disregarding God's Word or convictions. This dynamic is dependent on truth in the fellowship. We are not to be blind to corruption or abuse, for the Word of God clearly outlines the standards for leaders, including elders and deacons. *"Shepherd the flock of God ... willingly, not grudgingly, not for what you will get out of it. Don't lord over people but serve by your good examples. Younger men accept the authority of the elders. And all of you serve each other in humility*" (1 Pet. 5:2, NLT).

The example of a good Christian leader is showing that authority is based on service and not power (Matt. 20:25, 26; Mark 10:42–45). The safety comes because a good servant-leader is going to look out for his flock as he or she submits to God. He or she is going to follow the example of our Lord, the Good Shepherd. (John 10:11–18).

Ruth had come under the covering of Boaz, and he had great concern for her. In order that there would be no misunderstanding of her actions that night on the threshing floor, he cautions Ruth not to talk about it to protect her reputation. This may expose an impure motivation by Naomi to put Ruth in an undesirable situation in order to expedite a marriage proposal. By giving her grain to take back to Naomi, Boaz gives Ruth an excuse for coming to the floor. He is also showing her he is well able to care for her and Naomi (Ruth 3:14–15). In essence, Boaz is saying, "I've got you covered."

As leaders, spouses, and parents, it is our desire to want resolution for our loved ones. We want to see matters of concern put to rest. How much more does our heavenly Father want that for us (Matt. 6:25–34)? Naomi knows that Boaz, a man of great character, will not rest until the matter is taken care of.

There are also times when matters need to be put to rest with those in authority over us. No relationship is without times of conflict and confrontation, but how we respond to it is our choice. It can be hurtful and confusing, especially when we have given ourselves faithfully to a loved one, leader, or ministry. We may feel misunderstood, or we may not understand at all the actions or lack of action we feel is needed by the individual. We can continue on in relationship, pretending everything is okay, but inside there is turmoil. If you're like me, you muse about all you would do to remedy the situation.

I confess I have been faithful, but I have not always been loyal.

I have been faithful to people, faithful to carry out responsibilities, faithful to my word, but not loyal. *"Let your heart therefore be loyal to the Lord our God."* (1 Kgs. 8:61, NKJV). Loyal in this passage literally means "to be at peace.

> *¹⁰ Therefore I write these things being absent, lest being present I should use sharpness, according to the authority which the Lord has given me for edification and not for destruction. ¹¹ Finally, brethren, farewell. Become complete. Be of good comfort, be of one mind, **live in peace**; and the God of love and peace will be with you.* (2 Cor. 13:10–11, NKJV)

Lack of forgiveness, bitterness, and resentment all represent heart issues and cause one to be out of step with God's purpose for your life. You may see someone commit an action that is offensive, but it is no different than when you hold negative feelings in your heart against them. At times, we can be quick to address an issue before we confront the sin in our own hearts. It is important to ask the Lord for the right time to approach the person and doing what is necessary to make sure our heart is pure in the process. On the other hand, minimizing an offense is not healthy, either. Pretending it will go away or minimizing the situation might result in the offense taking deeper root, lying dormant until the right moment or situation awakens the seed to break through shallow soil.

Our words and actions are like seeds being sown in the soil of our hearts. Angry words, divisive actions, and over-the-top emotions are expressions of those pesky weeds that I am referring to. Good people will turn a blind eye to bad behavior (fruit) that not only hurts the individual but causes harm to the body of Christ. We may talk ourselves into believing that it really "isn't a big deal," but find as time goes on, we haven't been able to let go of the hurt. In the personal field of our heart, one weed is manageable, but left alone, they quickly multiply and choke out the desired greenery. In fact, we may continue to be attracted to behavior that yields similar fruit. Sadly, many families or ministries have found it necessary to return to a situation and deal with a crisis that initially started as a small problem. Honestly, I really dislike conflict, and over the years, I did everything it took to avoid it. I have had to learn that conflict resolution, approached in humility, can bring amazing results.

Conflicts like these are addressed in James 4. James is informing the readers that due to their jealousy, coveting, and unfaithful hearts to God, they don't receive all that He desires for them. All too often, lovely people will give in to not-so-glorious behavior. They repeat an offense disguised as a prayer request to make sure the story is not one-sided. Pride is clouding their ability to see the enemy at work and hindering grace from enabling them to victory. His admonition is profound and one that I have taken far too lightly at times and yet simple in application.

"Therefore submit to God. Resist the devil and he will flee from you" (James 4:7, NKJV). It is pretty straightforward, huh? But there is a nugget of truth in the word *submit*. We all are pretty familiar with the classic definition *to yield to authority,* but it is the second one that really brought me freedom:

> **Submit** (Websters): *2. present (a proposal, application, or other document) to a person or body for consideration or judgment.*

One morning, my attitude was taken to task as I heard the Lord say, "Submit your issues to me." I had been fixated on a situation that had happened many years before, and although I had forgiven all involved, I found myself with no peace. After a few moments had passed, I bowed my head and submitted the circumstance and realized in that sacred prayer that when I submit my hurts or ideas of how things should have occurred to God, I give the Lord the opportunity to be the righteous judge over it. All too often, I take control and plead my own case without having a complete perspective of the situation. When I am able to release my ideas of how it should work out and give God the ability to govern my life, it opens my eyes to see more than one side of the argument. The Lord will give us eyes of mercy for another person and with it, an opportunity to triumph over judgment. As we take these matters to the throne and allow the Lord to heal our hearts, Holy Spirit is able to settle the matter. Many times we misinterpret the scenario based on past concerns and failure in our life experience, twisted by an accuser, so that we may never have peace. Forgive, purposely cancel the debt of the transgression, bless, and trust the righteous Judge (Ps. 96:10), for He always will rule justly.

I am not advocating a blind loyalty that results in abuse of any kind or that we look away and do not confront wrongs committed. The Bible is very specific in how we approach this with the proper perspective and a reverence to assist in bringing restoration (Matt. 18:15–19). Loyalty means sticking by someone through a conflict and being at peace until there is a resolution. I know this can be difficult and have walked this out. Many years ago, my husband and I faced a difficult time in our marriage. I had every bit of ammunition to fight with (in the natural) at my disposal, but God had a different plan. I argued with the Lord on several occasions, trying to convince Him how faithful I was, but God knew what was in the deep places of my heart. I had coveted his position and nurtured it with resentment. Although, I had been faithful to my husband, I was not always at peace with his leading. That kind of conflict in my spirit led to an undermining of his leadership, that eventually brought compromise. My husband, being a mighty man of God, took responsibility and the necessary steps to walk in deliverance and change.

My part may have been more difficult. God required me to put a guard over my mouth. He spoke gently, but firmly, to use my words for intercession and not complaining. Father God explained that if I didn't, I would destroy my marriage. I spent many nights, while my family slept, pleading God's case for my marriage and my children. At times, symbolically, drawing a line in my carpet and speaking the blood of Jesus, telling the enemy that he was not allowed to cross it. It took a strong bridle over my mouth to keep me from pleading my own case, but had I voiced the turmoil brewing in my little mind, I would have forfeited the mighty deliverance that came. Praise God, not only did we experience deliverance, but restoration!

We can be faithful to God and man, and still allow our focus to be on the issue and not on God. There may be times that we are sharpening each other, yet the Lord needs to be our object of affection. We should be devoted to His ways so that we may be edified and not destroyed. Trusting God and loving people can be challenging even in the best of seasons. The truth is we are a people set apart for covenant, covered by Almighty God, bound in His love, and grafted in for purpose. We can be confident that as we wait on the Lord, He will settle the matter. It may involve action on our part or simply waiting to see Him save us out of a mess. So therefore, let us all humbly consecrate ourselves on the threshing floor.

Father,

Take my life; I consecrate myself afresh to You. I lay down all my dreams and all my concerns at Your feet, and I ask You to rule over the cares in my heart. Cover me and bind my desires to Your Word. Jesus, You are my advocate, and You will not rest until the matters of my life are settled. Thank you!

In Jesus's name, Amen.

Professions of Faith: Chapter 8

1. Read John 15:4–8 and explain the importance for us to be abiding in His presence.

_____

_____

_____

2. Read John 10:1–30 and outline the ways the Good Shepherd cares for His flock.

_____

_____

_____

3. Reflecting on the definition provided in this chapter, what is the difference between being loyal and faithful? Can they operate separately?

_____

_____

_____

Chapter 9
At the Gate of Redemption

Boaz went to the town gate and took a seat there. Just then the family redeemer he had mentioned came by, so Boaz called out to him, "Come over here and sit down, friend. I want to talk to you." So they sat down together. ² Then Boaz called ten leaders from the town and asked them to sit as witnesses. ³ And Boaz said to the family redeemer, "You know Naomi, who came back from Moab. She is selling the land that belonged to our relative Elimelech. ⁴ I thought I should speak to you about it so that you can redeem it if you wish. If you want the land, then buy it here in the presence of these witnesses. But if you don't want it, let me know right away, because I am next in line to redeem it after you."

The man replied, "All right, I'll redeem it."

⁵ Then Boaz told him, "Of course, your purchase of the land from Naomi also requires that you marry Ruth, the Moabite widow. That way she can have children who will carry on her husband's name and keep the land in the family."

⁶ "Then I can't redeem it," the family redeemer replied, "because this might endanger my own estate. You redeem the land; I cannot do it."

⁷ Now in those days it was the custom in Israel for anyone transferring a right of purchase to remove his sandal and hand it to the other party. This publicly validated the transaction. ⁸ So the other family redeemer drew off his sandal as he said to Boaz, "You buy the land."

⁹ Then Boaz said to the elders and to the crowd standing around, "You are witnesses that today I have bought from Naomi all the property of Elimelech, Kilion, and Mahlon. ¹⁰ And with the land I have acquired Ruth, the Moabite widow of Mahlon, to be my wife. This way she can have a son to carry on the family name of her dead husband and to inherit the family property here in his hometown. You are all witnesses today." (Ruth 4:1–10, NLT)

Would You Like to Go to Dinner?

The Sunday service was over, and my husband Paul and I were visiting with some friends and were just about to leave when a young man named Ryan, who our daughter had been seeing for a few years, asked us out to dinner. We agreed and set a time and place and proceeded to go home. Our daughter Chloe was on a missions trip to Uganda, so initially I thought he was just being nice, but as we got into to the car to leave, it occurred to us that he may have another question for us. We arrived at the restaurant, ordered our food, and after several minutes of small talk, Ryan nervously began to address the reason for our outing. Paul and I tried to hide our amusement as he stumbled over words until finally asking for our permission to marry our daughter. Honestly, this was a long time coming, but the dinner gesture was a nice touch. Of course we said yes, as we had prayed a long time for this day and had peace and assurance that the Lord was in this union. Later, through some other friends, we found out that Ryan was a little afraid of Paul. Perhaps this was due to a conversation they had early in their relationship where Paul explained to Ryan that Chloe is his princess and he expected him to treat her with respect and honor. In his heart, he may have questioned if he was up to the task. That was many years ago and as a husband and father to our grandchildren, Ryan has proved to be a worthy mate. We are blessed to have him as a part of our family.

Boaz goes up to the city gate and waits until the relative that is next in line to redeem Elimelech's estate walks by. Perhaps he is nervously pacing, rehearsing his cause. What will the relative say? Will he get the answer he is hoping for? Before we get into that, let us take a look at the significance of the gate.

The City Gate

The city gate was a gathering place for assemblies of people as they passed in and out of the city (2 Chron. 32:6). This led to using the gates for legal matters (Deut. 16:18), reading the law (Neh. 8:1–3), gathering news (Gen. 19:1), and gossiping (Ps. 69:12). Prophets were known to deliver their discourses and admonitions at the gate (Isa. 29:21; Jer. 17:19, 20; 26:10; Amos 5:10).

> *Gate* (Strong's H8179; 8176) *sha'ar*: opening, door. The primitive root is to split or open. It is also where we get the word *gatekeeper*.

The city gate was a place of legal transaction where people met to settled disputes and conversed about life. Prominent people would gather there. As I considered this, I couldn't help but think about early in my walk with the Lord and how hard it was for me to approach Father in relationship. Do I enter His gates with thanksgiving and praise? Do I have to say just the right things? Am I worthy enough? Have I sinned too much for Him to talk to me? And in reality, if I would to adhere to law alone, I am *not* worthy enough and my sin *is* too great. There was much to be nervous about, except that our Bridegroom and Shepherd made a way through His death and resurrection.

> *So he (Jesus) explained it to them: "I tell you the truth, I am the **gate** for the sheep,"* (John 10:9)

> *Jesus told him, "**I am the way,** **the** truth, and **the** life. No one can come to **the** Father except through me."* (John 14:6, NLT)

Family Court

Boaz calls a court session at the gate of the city. It is highly probable that he himself was an elder due to the fact that he was a man of great wealth, grandson of Nahshon (Prince of Judah), and a watchman over the fields. Boaz is eager to expedite the situation, not because of what he can receive from Ruth, but because of what he and his neighbors have discovered about her. She is a virtuous woman. *"Who can find a virtuous and capable wife? She is more precious than rubies."* (Prov. 31:10, NLT).

Boaz recognized Ruth's value as a woman of strength and integrity. It is at just the right moment, waiting by the gate, that the relative walks by. They discuss, along with ten elders, the issue at hand. Initially, the relative agrees to redeem the land of Elimelech until he learns it involves a marriage to Ruth. This could result in a situation where any son born to Ruth in that union would inherit the property, and it would no longer belong to the kinsman-redeemer. After counting the cost, the relative declines. We can only speculate why he declines, but possibly because it would confuse and alter any previous obligations or simply because he could not afford to purchase the land and acquire a bride. Boaz is now the kinsman-redeemer acquiring the estate and Ruth's hand in marriage.

In an act that was no longer practiced at the time of the book's inscription, a sandal was removed by the relative and given to Boaz. This act surrenders all rights of the property and allows his marriage to Ruth.

Symbolically, the foot or shoe in the Bible is used to demonstrate authority or possession. *"Wherever you set your **feet** the land will be yours"* (Deut. 11:24, NLT). Abram was told in Genesis 13:14–17 (NLT) to "take a walk in every direction and explore the new possessions I (the Lord) am giving you."

In Romans 4, we are told that **by faith,** we are sons and daughters of God like Abraham because it is **by faith** we have believed.

"Then He called His twelve disciples together and gave them power and authority over all demons, and to cure diseases. ² He sent them to preach the kingdom of God and to heal the sick" (Luke 9:1–2, NKJV). In a similar verse in Luke 10:19, Jesus gave the seventy (a number representing the Gentile nations) authority to trample on serpents and scorpions (representing spiritual enemies and demonic forces). Authority was given to the Jews, and because of Jesus, it was also given to the Gentiles. Ruth, back in chapter 1, had accepted the God of Naomi and had declared her faith in Him.

In spite of that, there is perhaps another reason the closer relative chose not to redeem Ruth. It may have been due to racial prejudice. She may have been discriminated against for being a Moabite.

Discrimination (Webster's): prejudiced or prejudicial outlook, action, or treatment. An act, practice, or instance of discriminating categorically rather than individually.

> *"But the law brings punishment on those who try to obey it (The only way to avoid breaking the law is to have no law to break)"* (Rom. 4:15, NLT).

> *"For whoever shall keep the whole law, and yet stumble in one point, he is **guilty** of all"* (James 2:10–13, NKJV).

Discrimination and prejudice make the assumption that if you are a certain ethnicity, look or act a certain way, are female, have a physical or emotional challenge, or you don't fit into the "culture" of the environment you belong to, then you are altogether lacking and therefore are disqualified. A person operating with a judgmental spirit will put standards on people that they themselves cannot live up to.

I confess at times I have a judgmental spirit.

I am the unwilling relative with a narrow view of circumstances and character. The purpose of the law was to show us our need for a savior, but in itself was unable to meet it (Rom. 7). We have all missed the mark, but through the redemptive work of Jesus, we have been justified freely by His grace. It is with that revelation we can allow each other the freedom to be all that He desires us to be.

The redeeming of Ruth by Boaz in marriage is a beautiful picture of what Christ ultimately completed for us (Gal. 3:26–29). Not only did He make a way; He brought peace in the transaction by breaking down and splitting walls of division between Jews (Boaz) and Gentiles (Ruth).

> *Don't forget that you Gentiles used to be outsiders. You were called "uncircumcised heathens" by the Jews, who were proud of their circumcision, even though it affected only their bodies and not their hearts. [12] In those days you were living apart from Christ. You were excluded from citizenship among the people of Israel, and you did not know the covenant promises God had made to them. You lived in this world without God and without hope. [13] But now you have been united with Christ Jesus. Once*

you were far away from God, but now you have been brought near to him through the blood of Christ.

*¹⁴ For Christ himself has brought **peace** to us. He united Jews and Gentiles into one people when, in his own body on the cross, he broke down the wall of hostility that separated us. ¹⁵ He did this by ending the system of law with its commandments and regulations. He made peace between Jews and Gentiles by creating in himself **one new people from the two groups**.* (Eph. 2:11–14, NLT)

By His grace we can allow those around us to walk in freedom by releasing them from our standards and expectations. Boaz (grace) took a risk and to redeem Ruth, one that the relative (law) was unwilling or unable to take. Jesus came in grace and truth to redeem each one of us, whereas the law was unable to fulfill the requirements. *"The Word became flesh **and** made his dwelling among us. We have seen his glory, the glory of the one **and** only Son, who came from the Father, full of **grace and truth**"* (John 1:14, NIV).

Root Systems

A few years ago, my husband and I were on a vacation in Maui, and while we were there, we took a hike. We walked through luscious greenery, viewing exquisite waterfalls and exotic flowers. At one point in the trek, I was following along and suddenly tripped over roots that had been exposed over years of erosion. Excessive weather conditions over time had stripped away the topsoil needed to protect the roots, leaving them vulnerable to the elements. As I studied the elaborate root systems, I believe the Lord impressed on my heart that it is easy to walk through life, ignoring external conditions that erode the truths that keep us anchored to our faith. Patterns of the world strip away beliefs connected to the intrinsic value of every human being. Little by little, what started as identifying unique qualities in a person become differences that the devil exploits resulting in greater division.

There is discrimination and prejudice on many levels still operating in society, and I will say that personally what I have experienced is minimal. I am in no way pretending to have all the answers, but my intention is to point out the foundational roots to why we act in horrible ways at times to precious individuals. We don't have to own exclusion, in fact, that is the opposite of what He displayed in His kingdom.

> *Make sure no outsider who now follows GOD*
> *ever has occasion to say, "GOD put me in second-class.*
> *I don't really belong."*
> *And make sure no physically mutilated person*
> *is ever made to think, "I'm damaged goods.*
> *I don't really belong."* (Isa. 56:2–3, MSG)

In God's kingdom, there is no one perfect race. Each one of us are created in His image with great purpose, and the enemy would want nothing more than to pervert that truth. We need to examine our hearts and ask why one would act in such a way toward someone God has already embraced. For myself, what is at the root is a little thing called "pride" that is a large part of the problem. Ignorance and insensitivity are other roots that entangle our ability to walk alongside people who are different than us. As Christ-followers, it is our responsibility to live, honor, and respect one another; for us to do anything else is dishonoring to God.

If you have experienced behavior that left you broken and feeling set aside, the Lord wants to see you restored. We can trust Him in times of hardship, suffering, unjust treatment, judgment, and bitter disappointment. It won't involve a magic act and may not resolve in an instant, but God has a purpose in it all!

> *"And we know that **all** things **work together** for **good** to those who love God, to those who are the called according to His **purpose**"* (Rom. 8:28, NKJV). Let's look more closely at some key words in this verse:
>
> ***Work together*** (Strong's G4903) *synergeo*: to cooperate or collaborate.
>
> ***Good*** (Strong's G18) *agathos*: physical and moral sense; aesthetically suggesting attractiveness and excellence.
>
> ***Purpose*** (Strong's G4286) *prosthesis*: pro, before and thesis, a place. It is an intention or deliberate plan.

When we cooperate with the Spirit of God, like Ruth, things will turn around, and redemption will come from unlikely places. Could it be that when you are in the worst situation imaginable, God would anoint you to speak life into someone else? Perhaps you could look at it this way: That missed job promotion, will prepare the way for God to collaborate with another company on your behalf, providing you a career that will bring success and a better future. The social activities where you were uninvited because of a physical disfigurement will actually attract you to relationships of substance.

When you finally realize that the enemy has lied to you about being unacceptable and come out of the isolation that has kept you bound, you may just be the missing piece to a problem, opening the door for others to walk in freedom. Obviously, it takes a lot of resolve to get to a place where you push back in grace and much healing to express love in the face of discrimination. These hurts are deep, but you are created for greater things!

A gate led to a pathway of redemption for Ruth, and it was not what was expected. It did not lead to a synagogue or even to the person closest to her; it was by God's plan. She had yielded to Him and good, "attractive" work was fulfilled by a faithful God (Phil. 1:6) at the gates of the city.

Father God,

I thank you for Your grace that is lavishly poured out through Your son, Jesus. I choose today to walk in it, not only for myself, but toward others, taking ground with the authority you have given. I want to see Your people as you see them, with eyes of love and freedom. I will declare to the brokenhearted and captive that Your plans are good, bringing ultimate purpose. I will not only declare it, but will receive it into my heart.

In Jesus's precious name, Amen.

Professions of Faith: Chapter 9

1. Read Proverbs 31:10–31 and list all the qualities Ruth possessed.

_____

_____

_____

_____

2. After reading Isaiah 26:1–9, what are some of your observations?

_____

_____

_____

3. What are some of the ways you and I can discriminate or act in judgment toward one another?

_____

_____

4. Read 1 Corinthians 10:23–32. What are some of the qualities expressed in living a life governed by grace?

_____

Chapter 10
A Blessed Lineage Restored

⁹ And Boaz said to the elders and all the people, "You are witnesses this day that I have bought all that was Elimelech's, and all that was Chilion's and Mahlon's, from the hand of Naomi. ¹⁰ Moreover, Ruth the Moabitess, the widow of Mahlon, I have acquired as my wife, to perpetuate the name of the dead through his inheritance, that the name of the dead may not be cut off from among his brethren and from his position at the gate. You are witnesses this day."

¹¹ And all the people who were at the gate, and the elders, said, "We are witnesses. The Lord make the woman who is coming to your house like Rachel and Leah, the two who built the house of Israel; and may you prosper in Ephrathah and be famous in Bethlehem. ¹² May your house be like the house of Perez, whom Tamar bore to Judah, because of the offspring which the Lord will give you from this young woman."

¹³ So Boaz took Ruth and she became his wife; and when he went in to her, the Lord gave her conception, and she bore a son. ¹⁴ Then the women said to Naomi, "Blessed be the Lord, who has not left you this day without a close relative; and may his name be famous in Israel! ¹⁵ And may he be to you a restorer of life and a nourisher of your old age; for your daughter-in-law, who loves you, who is better to you than seven sons, has borne him." ¹⁶ *Then Naomi took the child and laid him on her bosom, and became a nurse to him.* ¹⁷ *Also the neighbor women gave him a name, saying, "There is a son born to Naomi." And they called his name Obed. He is the father of Jesse, the father of David.*

¹⁸ *Now this is the genealogy of Perez: Perez begot Hezron;* ¹⁹ *Hezron begot Ram, and Ram begot Amminadab;* ²⁰ *Amminadab begot Nahshon, and Nahshon begot Salmon;* ²¹ *Salmon begot Boaz, and Boaz begot Obed;* ²² *Obed begot Jesse, and Jesse begot David.* (Ruth 4:9–22, NKJV)

While writing this book, my dear father-in-law went home to be with the Lord. The preceding days were filled with sweet times, sitting by his bedside singing old songs, praying, and reminiscing about his amazing conversion to Christ. Before the miraculous turnaround, his family was broken; an all-too-familiar story with which many of us can identify. In fact, my side of the family was somewhat of a mess before the grace of God, but piece by piece, He began healing the dysfunction of destructive patterns. Please don't misunderstand, I am not saying at all that we have arrived to completion. I am giving thanks to God's grace for bringing us closer to health.

Although each of us may have a similar story, we may not always have the benefit of seeing the blessing in it all. We might be the first person in our family to be pulled out of that miry pit and are just getting started in setting our feet firmly in the promises of God. It can be hard to see God's goodness in the middle of dysfunction and the consequences brought on by choices made out of broken souls. It can take time to see the redemption process in effect, but you can be sure it is. The work of the Cross of Jesus reaches back into our history and exchanges the curse of sin for God's gracious blessing. Our family was privileged to not only hear words of affirmation, but to see it lived out in tremendous grace, modeled in our precious dad.

A blessing declared over someone is a powerful thing! It is more than a phrase used after someone has sneezed or spoken flippantly in a "Bless you" as we leave an event. It has the power to change the course of life, if only to leave an impression in the mind of the recipient that they are simply *blessed*. In recent years, I have been convicted of the sacredness of a spoken blessing and, with intention, have declared it over others, especially loved ones.

By God's mighty plan, Boaz declares he is the redeemer of Elimelech's estate. Not only from a material place, but his name and position are restored. The elders and witnesses proclaim a blessing over Ruth and Boaz, releasing prosperity and implying future descendants. The Lord blesses their union with a son named Obed which completes the restoration and provides another link in the lineage of David, preparing a way for the Messiah-Redeemer.

The Blessing:

The blessing of God was a primary focus of His covenant relationships. Two statements were present when the blessing occurred. First, it was a public declaration of favor with God. Second, it bestowed the power for prosperity and success. Although the Biblical record begins with a blessing (Gen. 1:21–22) and the directive to be "fruitful," the curse was introduced early (Gen. 3:14). God countered the curse by declaring that through Abram all peoples on earth would be blessed. That would be accomplished through the nation of Israel.

Ceremonial Blessing:

- ❧ Family: the Father father blessed the wife and children. Genesis 27:27–29; 1Samuel 2:20
- ❧ Kingdom: the ruler blessed the subjects. 2 Samuel 6:18
- ❧ Tribe: the tribe of Levi was set apart to pronounce blessing. Deuteronomy 10:8; 21:5

Less Ceremonial:

- ❧ Those who walk in obedience are blessed with affluence and victory. Deuteronomy 28:1–14
- ❧ Those who walk in disobedience are cursed with consequences. Deuteronomy 28:15–68

God's promise to Abraham is a foundation for blessing in the New Testament and is fulfilled in the person of Jesus Christ (Gal. 3:8–14).

Believers are:

- ❧ Blessed with every spiritual blessing Ephesians 1:3
- ❧ Those who inherit promises from patriarchs Hebrews 6:12,15;12:17
- ❧ A source of blessing to the world, especially in response to persecution 1 Peter 3:9; Luke 6:27–28; Romans 12:14; 1 Corinthians 4:12

As we look at Ruth 4:10–12, we see a reference to lineage and the house of Israel. The family line is through the name of Rahab the prostitute, a Gentile, and the mother of Boaz. It is important because it shows us another story of redemption within the family history of the Messianic bloodline (Matt. 1:1–17). Through its history, God had charged Israel with unfaithfulness, even accusing them with prostitution on the threshing floor (Hos. 4:1; 8:1–8, 14; 9:1–9). Pretty intense!

God who is rich in mercy and abundant in grace has proven His redemption through the lineage of Jesus. He is reaching into the bloodline of Christ to resolve the roots of iniquity. I am not suggesting that Jesus had sin in His life, but His family line sure did. To prove further that God had a plan, it was prophesied hundreds of years before Christ.

> *There shall come forth a Rod from the stem of Jesse and a Branch shall grow out of his roots.* (Isa. 11:1–2, NKJV)

> *And out of that branch will come justice and righteousness.* (Jer. 23:5; 33:15)

Jesus has come from a damaged root system in order to restore it. We all have knots that disfigure our family tree. Most of us don't talk about it; we are marred with the shame of missteps in decisive moments. Early on in my walk with Lord, I really did not have a grasp of all that the Cross afforded. I was at peace with knowing my sins were forgiven and I had eternity security in heaven, but I had little understanding of magnitude of the work of Calvary. Splintering through my generations were lies, abuse, addictions, perversion, and, well, there may be more that I have yet to discover even now many years later. As I began to uncover deep-seated patterns, it almost became hopeless as to whether freedom was attainable.

"*But He was wounded for our transgressions, He was bruised for our iniquities*" *Isaiah 53:5, NKJV).* Many of us have claimed this beautiful prophecy of Jesus, as it pertains to the forgiveness of sin so that we could be restored to right relationship with the Father, but we have yet to lay hold of the entirety of it. To understand the complete work of the Cross, let's take a closer look at the original language.

Transgression (Strong's H 6586, 6588) *pesha':* a revolt, rebellion, sin. The root word is *paso* (H 6585) which means to stride.

Iniquity (Strong's H 5771) *avon*: perversity (i.e. moral), fault, mischief. The root word *avah* (H5753) is to make crooked. Iniquity can be connected to character and guilt.

Jesus not only shed His blood externally from His wounds, He shed His blood internally with a bruise. He covered the sin that we would walk out of the perversion or "crooked ways" in our family line. Families often claim bragging rights over a profession linked through the generations. Some examples include doctors, lawyers, pastors, and teachers, just to name a few. On the contrary, very few of us would like to discuss the skeletons in the closet of our homestead, the issues that are best kept secrets from anyone we may or want to influence in the future. The problem with that is they are still there, and we strive in our own strength to fight a battle that has already been won. Eventually, it will lead to captivity, enslaving us to the very sin we refused to recognize in our ancestors. There is freedom because the same blood that saved us from our sin we committed also delivers us from the patterns that lie in wait to ensnare us, eventually leading us to bondage. Confess it, appropriate His blood, and receive His grace. Calvary covered it all!

Unfortunately, knowing that and walking in it may be two different things, especially if you have wrestled with a habit or dysfunction for a long time. No matter what you call it, after a while, our identity is married to the habit, dysfunction, sin, or addiction, and shame keeps us from taking the name of that which we have become engaged.

Many heroes of the faith faced similar circumstances, specifically Jacob. We ultimately know him as one father of the Jewish people, but the course he took was littered with deception and betrayal.

Jacob was a twin born to Isaac and Rebekah. While his brother Esau's name meant "hairy," Jacob's name meant "deceiver" (Gen. 25:23–28). He began to walk out that description over his life (Gen. 27); when encouraged by his mother, he seized an opportunity to take the birthright from Esau. While Esau despised the blessing and sold his inheritance for a meal, Jacob took full advantage of the moment. Sin is always knocking at the door when we desire something that does not belong to us. Jacob misled his father Isaac by pretending to be Esau.

Thankfully, God had other plans and spoke to the future plans involving Jacob.

The Ladder to Success

> *¹⁰ Meanwhile, Jacob left **Beersheba** and traveled toward **Haran**. ¹¹ At sundown he arrived at a good place to set up camp and stopped there for the night. Jacob found a **stone** to rest his head against and lay down to sleep. ¹² As he slept, he dreamed of a stairway that reached from the earth up to heaven. And he saw the angels of God going up and down the stairway.*
>
> *¹³ At the top of the stairway stood the Lord, and he said, "I am the Lord, the God of your grandfather Abraham, and the God of your father, Isaac. The ground you are lying on belongs to you. I am giving it to you and your descendants. ¹⁴ Your descendants will be as numerous as the dust of the earth! They will spread out in all directions—to the west and the east, to the north and the south. And all the families of the earth will be blessed through you and your descendants. ¹⁵ What's more, I am with you, and I will protect you wherever you go. One day I will bring you back to this land. I will not leave you until I have finished giving you everything I have promised you."*
>
> *¹⁶ Then Jacob awoke from his sleep and said, "Surely the Lord is in this place, and I wasn't even aware of it!" ¹⁷ But he was also afraid and said, "What an awesome place this is! It is none other than the house of God, the very gateway to heaven!"*

> *¹⁸ The next morning Jacob got up very early. He took the **stone** he had rested his head against, and he set it upright as a memorial pillar. Then he poured olive oil over it. ¹⁹ He named that place **Bethel** (which means "house of God"), although it was previously called **Luz**.*
>
> *²⁰ Then Jacob made this vow: "If God will indeed be with me and protect me on this journey, and if he will provide me with food and clothing, ²¹ and if I return safely to my father's home, then the Lord will certainly be my God. ²² And this memorial pillar I have set up will become a place for worshiping God, and I will present to God a tenth of everything he gives me." (Gen. 28:12–22, NLT)*

Let us focus on some key words in this passage.

Beersheba (SH884): well of an oath.

Haran (SH2039, 2771): mountaineer, symbolically = promotion

Luz (SH3869, 3870): To depart, nut tree, probably almond, which is the awakener in scripture—the first to bud.

Stone (SH68): To build (root 1129), to repair, a midwife's stool.

Bethel (SH1008): House of God.

Just like in the lives of Jacob and Ruth, God will interrupt our path and take us from a place where we are making promises to be different, to actual change and promotion. He speaks His Word of covenant over us, waking us up to realize He is the God of our past, present, and future. The ascent up the ladder begins with recognition of who God is: the greater reason for the success. Our job is to consecrate our lives to Him and depart from what is comfortable, knowing in time He will birth new things by bringing spiritual midwives alongside to assist us on our journey of deliverance and purpose.

It is important to note that God lets Jacob know that one day, He will bring Jacob back to the land. So many times we run back to what we know instead of waiting for God's timing in the process. He is with us every step of the way, leading us on into promises. A quick return to the familiar may result in a setback and an undoing of the work in our character. *"You don't get character because you're successful; you build character because of the hardships you face"* (Herman Edwards, Head Coach Arizona State University).

We are to rest, not strive. Resting looks different, depending on the person and the season they are in. One may continue to serve, embracing a mind-set of rest while another may be altogether still, yet playing out in their mind ways to feel useful. I have been in either scenario, but when we allow rest to morph into futility the results can leave us discouraged.

I confess that I have felt unproductive and even barren.

When I was pregnant with our third child, complications arose to such an extent that I ended up delivering him ten weeks early. As he grew and became stronger and healthier, I couldn't shake the melancholy emotions that began to show up. I should have been rejoicing at the miracle God performed for our family, but instead I met with sadness. It took a while to feel somewhat normal again, but after a few years, I found myself expecting again, only this time at about thirteen weeks into the pregnancy, the baby died. Not only was I dealing with the loss of a precious life, it was compounded by the reality that I had not been able to carry life to term for our previous child. I walked through several months of grieving, not only the miscarriage, but also the interrupted pregnancy as well.

In those moments, the enemy magnified a situation many walk through, to an overwhelming feeling that my inability to carry life was related to my ability to be fruitful in other areas of my life. Satan will put the focus on the loss so that you might come into agreement with defeat! The enemy's purpose is to disqualify all that you had gained in the process. Satan's plan is to discount your lessons of faith and times when you learned to trust God through all the pain. In turn, God will give you peace, even when you lack the understanding of your circumstances.

As I learned what it meant to reclaim God's promises, I recognized that fruitfulness does not always mean accomplishment, and barrenness is not always empty. We must not forfeit the treasures from the darkness. If we are not careful, our continuously rehearsed sadness will grow into a monument to grief we revisit and memorialize but will never be completely healed from.

It certainly is easier to remember our recent days than to recall what happened many years earlier. Perhaps, we have chosen to forget, rather than face the pain of regret. We end up lost on the detour, distracted by cleverly placed landmarks the enemy staked to wipe out any attempt of arriving at our God-purposed destination. Satan disguises life lessons into life sentences of condemnation, all the while stealing time along the way. Through a series of bad choices and maybe even outright sin, our restoration road hits a roadblock, as we leave those dreams and desires off to the side, telling ourselves to just "let it go." That's when God will use things like a dream to remind us of who we are. It may even be the anniversary of that moment when everything came crashing down, not so we are discouraged by it but to fight for it. We must recognize the hurt and disappointment in ourselves or others and decide to not let the enemy steal from us any longer. Later days are greater, restitution is sure, and recompense is the divine payback for what was lost. God still knows you by your name and the original purpose for which you were created. Through the blood of Jesus, He only forgets the offense. He renames us to represent the cleansed work in our hearts, redeeming our lives. *"You shall no longer be termed Forsaken, nor shall your land any more be termed Desolate, but you shall be called **Hephzibah (His delight), ** and your land **Beulah (married)**"* (Isa. 62:4, NKJV).

Jacob was restored and given a new name and identity. God affirmed the blessing that was spoken earlier over Abram and called him Israel (Gen. 32:28), through a dream He renewed His covenant and established a people by calling to remembrance the original intent.

I believe in Christ we are new creations; the old is passed away—dead and gone—and new life is emerging (2 Cor. 5:17). We can do a disservice to those who are coming out of a dependency or dysfunction by continuing to tie their identity to the addiction. The Lord, many times in scripture, renamed the individual, wiping away the previous association with their name. He calls us "His delight," and where we have been recognized for deception, He calls forth destiny. While it is important to not continually name them, it is more crucial that they recognize their deliverance and the process of renewing the mind. This may take years of Holy Spirit reframing thought patterns with the Word of God, due to abuse and believing lies of the enemy.

The next important step is applying wisdom to our situation by not opening a door that would allow the stronghold to return. This happens by entertaining behavior leading to habits or allowing pride to come into our thinking that we have enough willpower to resist the temptations of our past haunts. Guarding yourself against such temptation involves giving yourself to accountability by building relationships out of transparency and honesty. There is risk involved because there are those who struggle with vulnerability, and after a conversation that involves divulging certain behavior or challenges, they may resist associating with you aside from mere pleasantries at the grocery store. However, I have found there are more people who desire a friendship filled with open dialog than those who hide behind their flawless demeanor.

The Blessing of Community

It is humbling to have walked down the road to redemption alone, but it is awe-inspiring to walk that road with others beside you. The women that pointed out Naomi's misery in the early chapters of Ruth came to recognize the complete turnaround in her heritage. They experienced her sadness but began to rejoice in God's goodness.

> *[14] Then the **women** said to Naomi, "Blessed be the LORD, who has not left you this day without a close relative; and may his name be famous in Israel! [15] And may he be to you a restorer of life and a nourisher of your old age; for your daughter-in-law, who loves you, who is better to you than seven sons, has borne him." (Ruth 4:14–15, NKJV)*

We enjoy the blessing of community when we surround ourselves with fathers of faith, those who raise us up to levels of belief through trusted words and leadership. At the same time, spiritual mothers act as midwives, assisting in the birth of dreams and acquired inheritance. What it comes down to is that we need each other. Community is more than social interaction in a close proximity; it is interaction where we are building something together that supersedes accomplishment. It is kingdom-minded and presence-driven, resulting in fulfilling God's purposes. We put our hands to the plow to prepare for a righteous harvest, and together we will enjoy the first fruits. We will experience growth, not only seen with our eyes, but with our spirits, bearing witness to a mighty work of God.

Blessing Through the Hurt

A more challenging aspect for me, walking the walk of faith, is blessing those who have hurt me or a member of my family. It can be a downside when being part of a community of believers. I may be able to forgive and release them of any emotional debt, but taking it a step further and blessing them? It is easier said than done! Why should I bless someone who has caused me pain, and why would God ask me to? After all, hasn't He walked me through the process of forgiveness already and knows how hard it was to just do that?

> *27 "But to you who are **willing to listen**, I say, love your enemies! Do good to those who hate you. **28 Bless those who curse you. Pray for those who hurt you. 29** If someone slaps you on one cheek, offer the other cheek also. If someone demands your coat, offer your shirt also. **30** Give to anyone who asks; and when things are taken away from you, don't try to get them back. **31** Do to others as you would like them to do to you.* (Luke 6:27–37, NLT)

This is a strong word for even the most compliant of us—so much so that Jesus differentiates between those who would listen and those who would take a hard pass on what He is saying to them. Are you willing to consider what Jesus is teaching us to do? I am struck by the word *willing*. We have a choice, loved ones, and that choice involves our will to do the work of the Father. I am reminded of John the Baptist and the portion of scripture he is so known to declare, *"He must increase, but I must decrease"* (John 3:30). John's words to us are more than a powerful statement; they are truth he lived out until he was completely diminished by death. John not only knew his place, he knew his purpose. Right before that well-known verse, John says: *"He who has the bride is the bridegroom; but the friend of the bridegroom, who stands and **hears him**, rejoices greatly because of the bridegrooms voice. Therefore this joy of mine is fulfilled"* (vs. 29). It is not joyful to bless those who abused, talked badly about us, behaved indifferent, or were careless with their actions, but it establishes the kingdom. It allows God to bring the necessary parameters needed in order to rightly bless them. At the same time, it keeps our hearts near His heart, listening intently to what *He* would say about the matter. We may decrease, but Jesus is increasing in our hearts, souls, minds, and strength. Our willingness to not only listen, but to act by blessing through the pain, exposes the depth of our friendship with Him.

Who Gives This Woman?

Boaz and Ruth were married; she had a new name, new identity, and a new family. Ruth 4:13 reads: "The Lord gave her (Ruth) conception." Scholars believe that this reference may hint to the possibility that Ruth may have been infertile while married to Mahlon due to the fact that several years of marriage had never yielded an offspring. God gave Ruth a new life and a new husband, and now a little baby completes the circle of restoration. What began as a commitment to follow Naomi to unfamiliar land, with no guarantee of acceptance, relationship, or provision, yielded all of that and more. Lack is replaced by fruitfulness and a barren womb with life. What began as a complete loss has now been recovered.

Blessing came to the house of Elimelech, with his lineage restored.

Abraham was the father of Isaac.
Isaac was the father of Jacob.
Jacob was the father of Judah and his brothers.
³Judah was the father of Perez and Zerah (whose mother was Tamar).
Perez was the father of Hezron.
Hezron was the father of Ram.
⁴Ram was the father of Amminadab.
Amminadab was the father of Nahshon.
Nahshon was the father of Salmon.
*⁵Salmon was the father of **Boaz** (whose mother was Rahab).*
***Boaz** was the father of **Obed** (whose mother was **Ruth**).*
***Obed** was the father of Jesse.*
*⁶**Jesse** was the father of **King David**.*

A Blessed Lineage Restored

David was the father of Solomon (whose mother was Bathsheba, the widow of Uriah).
⁷ Solomon was the father of Rehoboam.
Rehoboam was the father of Abijah.
Abijah was the father of Asa.
⁸ Asa was the father of Jehoshaphat.
Jehoshaphat was the father of Jehoram.
Jehoram was the father of Uzziah.
⁹ Uzziah was the father of Jotham.
Jotham was the father of Ahaz.
Ahaz was the father of Hezekiah.
¹⁰ Hezekiah was the father of Manasseh.
Manasseh was the father of Amon.
Amon was the father of Josiah.
¹¹ Josiah was the father of Jehoiachin and his brothers (born at the time of the exile to Babylon).
¹² After the Babylonian exile:
Jehoiachin was the father of Shealtiel.
Sheltie was the father of Zerubbabel.
¹³ Zerubbabel was the father of Abiud.
Abiud was the father of Eliakim.
Eliakim was the father of Azor.
¹⁴ Azor was the father of Zadok.
Zadok was the father of Akim.
Akim was the father of Eliud.
¹⁵ Eliud was the father of Eleazar.
Eleazar was the father of Matthan.
Matthan was the father of Jacob.
*¹⁶ Jacob was the father of **Joseph, the husband of Mary**.*
*Mary gave birth to **Jesus**, who is called the **Messiah**.* (Matt. 1:2–16, NLT)

There are times in our life when it is easier to believe for someone else and rejoice in their good fortune, but this is for us too! We look at someone's situation and see a way out, but then we close the door to hope on ourselves. God does not show favoritism (Acts 10:34–35), doing for one and ignoring the needs of others. The genealogy of Jesus shows the Father's consistency in a bloodline of promise. It also shows the grace to work in imperfect people. There are those listed who are less than exemplary, and yet there they are. The list displays the broken, lost, troubled, sinful, liars, and prostitutes. Some of them were young and unqualified, and some were old and disqualified, but all were redeemed—all having purpose to fulfill God's plan. Why? Because our God, who promised, is *faithful* (Heb. 10:23)! He is faithful to deliver, redeem, restore, heal, correct, provide, equip, and a lot more.

Maybe you need to cry out to Him in a new, fresh way. Perhaps, in your eyes you are too far gone to be penciled into God's lineage. Shame is keeping you from receiving the hope that your life can change. Please hear this in your spirit: Jesus knows how to spell your name. You are more than the disappointment that is shaping your perspective. Trust Him and take a risk, leaving your spiritual Moab. Call upon God's grace to enable you to leave the place of lack that has filled you with sadness. Submit yourself to God and allow Holy Spirit to blow upon the hard places of your heart. The gentle breeze of the Spirit will prepare your heart for the seed of His Word. What you begin by faith, Jesus has already followed through in action. The sacrifice of Jesus on the Cross was complete, and His blood covers every sin and disappointment. We can certainly count on him—His name is faithful and true!

In the fields of Boaz, Ruth served with purpose. She trusted in the words of Naomi and believed in the provision of a faithful God. Now, she is seeing increase. The blessing of a precious son, Obed, is ushering in a new bloodline of promise. The blessing is for all of us. Will you ask Father God to speak His words of kindness over you? Will you allow the complete work of Jesus to restore the broken places of your heart and your family? The book of Ruth is more than just a story, it was a set-up. A staging for the most miraculous biography ever written—the life of Jesus! The prophecy is fulfilled in Jesus Christ, the Messiah and our Kinsmen-Redeemer.

Father,

I thank you for Jesus, for the plan of redemption so complete that I can be restored. You make a way beyond my own abilities or even ideas.

Forgive me for not resting when You have called me to, for not believing in the full promise of Your written Word. I not only forgive those who have hurt me, I also choose to bless them.

I embrace the destiny that You have for me and commit to declaring Your Word over my barrenness and trusting You with ever-progressing increase. You, Lord, are faithful to Your Word.

In Jesus's name, Amen.

Professions of Faith: Chapter 10

1. In Isaiah 53:2–5, we focused on how the blood of Jesus cleansed our sin and iniquity. What other provisions were made for us because of Jesus's complete sacrifice?

_____

_____

2. Read Deuteronomy 30:15–20. What has been set before us, and what are we to do?

_____

_____

3. In Ruth 4:14, we read about the rejoicing over God's redemptive work in the life of Ruth and Naomi. Read Romans 12:6–16, and write your observations of what it means to be part of a community of believers.

_____

_____

Bibliography

Bakers Evangelical Dictionary of Biblical Theology, http://www.biblestudytools.com/dictionary/meekness/

Boaz, http://www.abarim-publications.com/Meaning/Boaz.html#.Vypn_Y-cGNM

Book of Ezra, http://www.bible-history.com/old-testament/bookofezra.html

Exell, Joseph S., comps. and eds. *The Biblical Illustrator*, Vol. 23, Grand Rapids, MI: Baker Books, 1975, 1977.

Hayford, Jack W., New Spirit Filled Life Bible (NKJV), Nashville: Thomas Nelson, 2002.

Life Application Study Bible (New Living Translation), Carol Stream, IL: Tyndale House, 1996, 2004, 2007.

Merriam-Webster.com Dictionary, https://www.merriam-webster.com/dictionary. s.v. "discrimination," "submit," Accessed 30 Mar. 2020.

"Silent Night," http://www.toptenz.net/top-10-acts-kindness-world-war-2.php

Strong, James, LL.D., S.T.D., *The New Strongs Complete Dictionary of Bible Words*, Nashville: Thomas Nelson Publishers, 1996. s.v. as follows:

Ch.1 "confess"; "groaning"
Ch. 2 "dwell"; "Uzziah";
Ch. 3 "ashamed"
Ch.4 "estrangement"

Ch. 6 "Redeemer"
Ch 8 "Wing"; "wait"
Ch. 9 "Gate"; "work together"; "Good"; "Purpose"
Ch. 10 "Transgression"; "Iniquity"; "Beersheba"; "Haran"; "Luz"; "Stone"; "Bethel"

Unger, Merrill F., *Unger's Bible Dictionary*, Moody Press, Chicago, IL, 1957,1961,1966. The Moody Bible Institute of Chicago Third Edition, Thirty-third Printing, 1981

"Uniqueness of tears," http://www.dailymail.co.uk/sciencetech/article-3147892/The-crying-game-Photographer-captures-beautiful-microscopic-images-friend-s-tears-unique.html

Useem, Michael, "Fighting Fire with Fire," https://www.scribd.com/doc/46111667/The-Leadership-Moment-Wagner-Dodge-Mann-Gulch

CPSIA information can be obtained
at www.ICGtesting.com
Printed in the USA
LVHW080008211020
669148LV00017B/200